Running a Successful Rough Shoot

· RUNNING ·
A SUCCESSFUL
ROUGH SHOOT

Norman Mursell

Foreword by John Anderton

BLANDFORD PRESS
POOLE · NEW YORK · SYDNEY

*To all my sporting friends of the past
and present to whom I owe so much and
to the young sportsmen in whose hands
the future largely rests.*

*First published in the UK 1986 by Blandford Press
Link House, West Street, Poole, Dorset BH15 1LL*

Copyright © 1986 Norman Mursell

*Distributed in the United States by
Sterling Publishing Co, Inc,
2 Park Avenue, New York, NY 10016*

*Distributed in Australia by
Capricorn Link (Australia) Pty Ltd
PO Box 665, Lane Cove, NSW 2066*

British Library Cataloguing in Publication Data

Mursell, Norman
    Running a successful rough shoot.
    1. Hunting—Great Britain
    I. Title
    799.2'13   SK185

ISBN 0 7137 1762 7

Typeset in 11/14 pt 'Monophoto' Ehrhardt by Keyspools Ltd, Golborne, Lancashire

Printed in Great Britain

CONTENTS

| FOREWORD | 6 |

1·JANUARY	7
2·FEBRUARY	20
3·MARCH	34
4·APRIL	50
5·MAY	64
6·JUNE	79
7·JULY	94
8·AUGUST	105
9·SEPTEMBER	115
10·OCTOBER	125
11·NOVEMBER	136
12·DECEMBER	146

| INDEX | 160 |

FOREWORD

Norman Mursell is one of shooting's great ambassadors. His detailed and practical knowledge will be valued by any sportsman involved with the running of a game shoot. 600,000 people in Britain gain pleasure from their sport in a myriad of different ways. It is an honour to be invited to write this foreword to a book which will contribute to the benefit of the countryside, its wildlife and everything that the true sportsman holds dear.

The gamekeeper's place in rural life is hard to underestimate. If this book can be read by members of the non-sporting public they will understand a little more about game conservation and perhaps understand the way in which it has contributed to the wider conservation of our national heritage.

JOHN ANDERTON o.b.e.
Director – The British Association
For Shooting and Conservation

1 · JANUARY

J ANUARY IS THE MONTH when rough shooters and syndicates should take stock, assessing the number of birds remaining on the shoot. It is usually a good plan to refrain from shooting hen birds after the Christmas activities, in the hope that the coming breeding season will be a successful one. If hen birds have to be caught for laying purposes, as many small shoots do these days, it is still a good thing to have some birds on the ground to produce their own broods. This creates more interest out of the shooting season and a greater incentive to predator control. So often, this matter is not really carried out to the degree it should be. Very few unkeepered shoots have a 'gun' resident on the shoot so this entails extra effort by the people who enjoy the sport during the winter months.

Hopefully the season has been an enjoyable one, with plenty of birds and plenty of good sporting shots and, hopefully without any incidents to mar the pleasure. It is remarkable that there aren't more accidents in the shooting field, but maybe a lot of minor ones are only known to those actually involved. One incident which I recall shows how easily accidents can happen. On this occasion, which happened many years ago, a gamekeeper received a pellet in the cheek, a ricochet from a shot at a woodcock by a Duke, who was always most particular about gun safety. This unfortunate incident could have cost the keeper the loss of an eye, but instead he received a case of whisky and a case of champagne from a most apologetic employer!! This incident recalls

Woodcock.

what the old keeper said when asked how he had reached the age of ninety. 'I always falls flat on my face when I hear the shout "woodcock".'

Do make sure every shot you take is a safe one. Shooting at a target amongst trees is a potentially dangerous one when beaters or other guns are approaching. Surely one more bird in the bag is not worth a person injured, no matter how slightly.

Between drives, make sure the gun is unloaded and preferably 'broken', particularly when getting over fences. No apologies for repeating all the above, for you still see some inexperienced people treating a gun more like a walking stick!

In many places pigeons do not seem so plentiful as they were in the past. Anyone can hazard a guess why, but it is certainly not because larger numbers have been shot. Many years ago it was not unusual for guns to kill 50 or 60 after an evening shooting them coming in to roost. In most places, five or six per gun is more likely to be the number today.

Maybe pigeon shooting is not organised like it used to be, when vast areas of countryside would have a gun in every wood and spinney, keeping the blue hordes on the move until it became dark and they had to settle somewhere. Normally, this organised pigeon shooting took place after the pheasant-shooting season came to a close. On small shoots, if you have pigeons roosting in the area, why not have a go at them after a day's sport with the pheasants?

By January, game birds will be getting thin on the ground and it will not take quite as long to go through the coverts. If pigeon shooting is decided on, finish fairly early in the afternoon. It might be as well to have some refreshment, even if only liquid, before proceeding to where the pigeons are coming in to roost. The favourite roost is a wood comprised mainly of softwoods, particularly if a proportion of the trees are Norway spruce. Pigeons love to roost in well 'furnished' spruce where they are out of sight and presumably warmer for the night. Fortunately from the shooter's point of view, the birds usually drop into an open tree nearby before taking up their quarter for the night.

Don't all crowd into the wood which pigeons are known to favour. All may get a couple of shots, but the result will be to drive the birds away. Few, if any, will return that evening. Those that do usually drop like a stone from a great height straight into a dark spruce, making an almost impossible target for the waiting gun. It is much better if the guns spread themselves out over the woods available. A shot or two will send the birds away from their normal roost and, although they usually circle round, often high over head, they will eventually settle in adjoining woods. Guns waiting there then get a chance of a shot.

Often a lot of patience is required. Sometimes pigeons come in to roost early, probably because they have been feeding fairly close to the roost and have spent an undisturbed day gorging themselves, maybe on a field of kale or clover. Another time, it may be quite late before the birds appear, as they have had to travel some distance from the feeding grounds.

Weather is a big factor when shooting pigeons coming in to roost. Really rough weather keeps the birds much lower, which makes them an easier target – if pigeons ever are an easy target!

On one occasion, a keeper was shooting pigeons on an evening when it was blowing a gale. He swears he shot at a pigeon travelling

9

downwind and killed a following bird at least 10 yards behind! Quite likely true, and a story to bear in mind when shooting pigeon on a really rough night.

Hopefully you will all have some sport and be able to have a feed of pigeon as a change from pheasant and duck! One tip: as soon as you have collected the birds you have shot, empty the crops by nicking with a knife. Sometimes the crops burst when the pigeon hits the ground, but if you make sure all the vegetable matter is removed, the flesh will not be tainted when the time comes to have it on a plate.

What's nicer than casseroled pigeon breasts or a lovely crusty pigeon pie? You no doubt prefer a nice pheasant 'butty' well salted, but at least pigeon has a different flavour and could save buying a joint of beef!

*   *   *

I recall one January when almost everywhere experienced a period of severe weather. Very low temperatures and heavy falls of snow caused quite a reduction in organised shooting days. However, so long as game birds can get an adequate supply of food, very few are likely to die in these arctic conditions. Should the weather turn severe, it is well worth while ensuring that all hoppers are kept topped up. If you are fortunate enough to be able to hand feed your birds, don't let the weather deter you from the daily chores! Most shooting men are pretty hardy types so the weather shouldn't prevent the essential tasks.

Should the snow lie very deep on the ground it is not easy to get about. Under such conditions, most pheasants will be close to a feeding point, making it much easier to see what stock is left on the shoot. An effort to at least visit the shoot is well worth while. A day's shooting in the snow may well be a different thing, but if only a comparatively light fall has taken place it may be a very productive operation. The pheasants will tuck in under the snow when disturbed at this time of year, so any woods must be driven slowly. Dogs being used to flush the birds must be reliable and not prone to pulling them out of the snow-covered herbage by the tail. A dog with a tendency to 'point' the game is useful under these conditions and, so long as the owner has full control, he can then flush the bird himself over the waiting guns. Nine times out of ten, a dog that 'pins' a bird is rather hard in the mouth and there is nothing worse than having to pluck and dress game that has been crushed in this manner.

In the old days, these damaged birds usually found their way into the kitchen of the 'big house', along with various other items from the game larder. Maybe there would be a duck or two, a hare, a few rabbits and pigeons, and these items were turned into a most delicious game pie. It is a long time since I tasted a pie like those made in the big-house kitchens of pre-war days. Many of the items used in the making of the pie had no doubt been hanging in the larder for quite a few days and were getting on the 'high' side, but they produced a mouth-watering meal. Many estates provided the gamekeepers with lunch on a shooting day and often game pie was on the menu. Today, with deep freezers, very little game is hung in the larder for long. Even after a couple of years on ice, a pheasant still tastes good but those subtle flavours found in a bird that has only been hung for a week are missing. So maybe the game pies of today are either made from game out of the freezer or freshly-killed items. In any case unless it is age or memory, they don't taste the same as in by-gone days!

Rabbits were mentioned as being in the game pies, but of course there aren't as many about as in those days of yesteryear. Some places have a greater build-up than others. In many cases, rabbits are spending most of their lives above ground, which is probably why they have suffered less from 'myxy'. Where they are going to ground, a lot of sport can be had ferreting.

There are several ways to use ferrets and these depend a lot on the various situations and conditions. If the rabbits are using burrows amongst a fair number of game birds, it is not advisable to shoot, at least during the shooting season. Pheasants are more important than rabbits anyway. Thus the method to adopt is 'purse netting'. This can be very successful if there are quite a number of rabbits to ground, but if the burrow is large and is home to only one or two rabbits it is really useless to try and net them. If it is intended to ferret a burrow using purse nets, it is often a good idea to have a look round a week or so before the day fixed and quietly trim back any briars and move any twigs that would hinder the nets. At the same time, make a mental note

Ferreting.

of the number of holes and, in particular, the position of a bolt-hole – there will be one, in fact often more than one!

Thus the ground is prepared for the day's sport. On the day, do not go near the burrow until the ferrets are ready for action, which means 'muzzled'. To bolt rabbits, the old keeper always used ferrets that had been muzzled and this was usually done before leaving home by using two short pieces of string with two knots in the middle about an inch or so apart. The gap between the two knots was placed over the ferret's nose and the ends tied round the animal's neck. Today, metal muzzles are readily available and so much easier to apply. Also, there is less risk of getting bitten!

Always make sure when you approach a burrow that you do so upwind. It is much better, unless it is a very large burrow, for one person to place the purse nets over the holes. The least possible noise should be made so that the occupants are not alerted. Once all holes are netted, the ferret may be slipped quietly into one of them and, with a bit of luck, the conies should bolt freely. Be patient and quiet. It can take a while for bunny to decide to leave!

If it is possible or advisable to shoot, the purse nets can be dispensed with but the same method of approach should be adopted. If at all possible none of the guns should stand in such a position that their scent can be carried to the rabbits below ground. Many people prefer to use unmuzzled ferrets when shooting, but this can be a disadvantage. Admittedly, when the ferret can nip, the cony is more likely to move, but very often the rabbits are driven to a dead end within the burrow and an 'open-mouthed' ferret will kill and start to eat one. This can either mean a long wait or a lot of digging.

A 'line' ferret has to be used to dig out a laid-up ferret and generally a large unmuzzled male is used for this purpose. Today, electronic aids are available to attach to ferrets. This makes it possible to locate their position below ground, a bit like using a metal detector. This doesn't make it much easier, except maybe to reduce the amount of digging to be done.

It is possible to use a line ferret only and, in this case, a purse net or two should be placed over likely holes and any others stopped up. It can be a rather unrewarding way of ferreting where the burrows are in sandy soil and are often deep and extensive. In clay, a lot of burrows are quite shallow and by 'lining' these a quite productive hour or so can be had.

One more proven suggestion and that is about the care of ferrets, particularly 24 hours before you are going to use them. Make sure the ferrets you are going to use 'loose' are fed, in order to reduce the risk of one getting 'laid up' and, to make the ferret to be used on a line that much keener, do not feed it a day before use.

Good luck with the rabbiting. May they all bolt and, if you have to dig, may the holes be shallow and the task be fruitful.

*   *   *

The months of October, November, December and January simply fly and the shooting season will soon be drawing to a close. No doubt most shoots will have decided on the programme for the next season. The amount of cash available for the rearing of pheasants, or maybe ducks and partridge, will dictate the number of birds reared. Feed is so expensive these days that it is not always easy to estimate the amount of money required to rear a given number of pheasants.

Labour too is expensive. Should a full-time gamekeeper or even a part-time helper have to be paid, this limits the funds for the essential feed. I must say here, as a retired keeper, that unless the workforce is well looked after, one cannot expect the best results when the shooting season comes round again.

Most full-time gamekeepers expect a suit of clothes a year and often waterproof clothing to keep dry in inclement weather. Transport is essential and a Land Rover is often the only suitable vehicle. In these days, a cottage more or less central to the shoot is needed and, from the wife's point of view, a modernised one at that!

All in all, quite a sum of money has to be allowed before the number of birds to be reared can even be thought of. We are referring to a shoot employing a professional gamekeeper and, if the money is available, there is no doubt it will certainly pay dividends. With a keeper resident on the shoot, there is much greater control of predators, giving the wild game a chance, and much less chance of trespassing, whether by poachers or others. Later in the season, a gamekeeper will drive the birds back from the boundaries and feed them in the desired places, thus ensuring good sport.

Many smaller syndicates cannot afford this rather expensive labour but can still, by good management, enjoy good sport. Plans must be made in January to ensure that things run smoothly during the rearing period in the spring. If it is decided to rear the birds amongst the syndicate members, and also to produce what eggs are required, whether to hatch or send off for hatching, January is a good time to collect hen birds for laying. Some shoots keep the laying stock penned all winter, never having released them, which is a good but expensive way. When you think that it takes almost 1 hundredweight of wheat to feed 100 hens a week, you can estimate the cost of keeping birds from August till January! It's no use using inferior feed for the results will surely be seen come hatching time.

Catching the stock needed after the shooting season is probably the most popular method, but I think it is probably advisable to get what hens you need in January and then you will have a better idea of the stock left when shooting ceases.

Should you be using the former method and keeping stock permanently penned, I would still advise catching what cock birds are

Trap for catching up hen pheasants to use as breeding stock.

needed in January. Cock birds which have been released and have survived through a shooting season always seem more virile than cocks kept penned. One more point: try and catch them where they were originally released. If they have remained at home after many disturbances and frights, you may just help to breed birds that are not quite so inclined to wander.

January is a social time for many of the shooting fraternity, both by the days of shooting held late in the month, when the sport is more for fun than the bag likely to be obtained, and for the many get-togethers that take place during the evenings.

Now is the time to let the willing unpaid helpers have a shot or two at the by now really wily birds. They may not kill many, but will have a whale of a time. No doubt there will be a lot of leg-pulling. 'When are you going to the blacksmith to get those barrels straightened?' is a remark I've heard more than once. I recall one occasion when, at lunchtime, a certain chap's cartridge bag had several cartridges added, of the same brand, but loaded with confetti! On complaining to his friends, all he got was 'Well for what you've killed today, paper is

15

plenty heavy enough to send after the birds'. All good-humoured fun of course, and usually taken in the right spirit. It would be a bad thing should any ill-temper enter into a sport with such lethal things as guns being carried.

Maybe a warning here may not come amiss. No matter how good natured the host or hosts may be, do not be too generous with the drinks at lunchtime. Those shooting may be used to a tipple or two, but one bought over the bar and of a given measure. Shooting lunches are a different kettle of fish. The drink is often poured straight out of the bottle into a fairly large glass, so it is difficult to know the amount drunk. I have, once or twice, on such occasions, seen men shooting who should not have had a gun in their hands. Please be careful, but I don't suggest being mean.

The evening social occasions are usually very pleasant affairs. Perhaps a film show is arranged to give an insight into other sporting activities, not only in this country but from abroad as well. The Wildfowlers' Club organise many of these events and, in most cases, non-members are made very welcome. I have been delighted to be a guest at a number of these functions and some of the films shown have been really remarkable. The sight of vast numbers of geese on the wing is really awe-inspiring. This was an American film, of course, but the splendour of the scenery and the number of wildfowl in the air kept all eyes glued to the screen.

I understand a large number of films, all with a sporting theme, are held by the British Association for Sport and Conservation and are available for hire by *bona-fide* sporting organisations. If you haven't seen any of them, I strongly recommend that you make every effort to do so.

The above are all really end-of-season activities. By now you should all have had a good season's sport and be planning for the season that, at the moment, seems so far away. It will come sure enough, but don't forget, the effort you put into planning your sport now, will show when the time comes. A gamekeeper, to be successful, has to be dedicated to his job, and folks that have to do their own keepering have to be dedicated too!

*   *   *

The end of the game-shooting season is fast approaching. Hopefully it has been an enjoyable one for all those connected with the sport. There are so many good folk who have a great interest in shooting in the field but are unable to afford to shoot. Large shoots, small shoots, syndicates and even rough shoots depend at least to some degree on the help, often unpaid, of these 'volunteers'. Maybe it's a farm worker who is keeping his eye on an area of rough shooting when the person holding the sporting rights lives miles away. Then there are the beaters on the small shoot, usually paid only a nominal sum, for the shoot has to be run as economically as possible. Such beaters have to have a keen interest in shooting or else they would not, as is often the case, lose a day's pay for a pound or two beating, often in foul conditions. There are also the 'dog men' who attend these shoots, either to help flush the birds out of thick cover or to pick up the game, particularly the wounded birds when a drive is completed. Some 'dog men' are only too pleased to render such a service, for they are in the business of breeding and training gundogs and a day's sport picking up at shoots can be to their advantage. It gives them an opportunity to work their dogs under field conditions and, of course, a chance to meet potential customers. These dog trainers, though in the minority, are welcome at a shoot, not only for the high standard of their dogs' work, but also because it gives an opportunity for, shall we say, 'men with dogs' to see what a well-trained dog is capable of. We must not forget the old lad, and it is often an old-timer, probably not capable of a day's beating through rough cover, who looks after the game when it has been shot. He nevertheless enjoys every minute on the game cart.

All worthy men these but, you may say, what about the keeper? Well it is really the keeper who depends upon such men, for few estates employ enough labour to provide enough men for even a small shoot. I did say in many, nay, probably most cases, the beaters receive remuneration that bears little resemblance to what their labours are worth. I also say, but perhaps all won't agree, that this is a good thing. If, the pay for a day's beating is equal to, or above, an average day's pay, an element would almost certainly creep in who weren't particularly interested in the sport. Should this happen, it would make the keeper's job more difficult and lead to a lower standard.

In view of the foregoing, why not try and encourage those people who give such good service during the shooting season, by providing them with the opportunity for a little shooting enjoyment. It is quite obvious that not all, or for that matter many, shoots can give such men a day's pheasant shooting. Some can arrange a day at the end of the season to kill cocks only, what a chance to let your invaluable helpers have a go! The bag may only be twenty birds all day, but those men will talk about it for a long while, and by the way, don't forget to give them a good feed at lunchtime! Such a day can only be to the advantage of the shoot.

Such a day probably cannot be arranged on the smaller and rough shoots, but there are almost certain to be pigeons coming to roost in your woods. Give all your helpers who want to (they won't all) the chance to go pigeon shooting at roosting time. As a rule, pigeons favour one or two woods more than others and I suggest that you draw lots for who is to go where, and that it is arranged for each gun to move to the next wood on the next week. Saturday afternoon is probably the best time to arrange it, for few of these interested folk are likely to want

Pigeon shoot at Terling, Essex, 1950.

to go to a football match. It won't do any harm to give them a box of cartridges apiece and, at the same time, remind them that there are a few carrion crows and magpies about! It might be as well to catch a few stock birds up before you make such arrangements but, unless there are large numbers of hen birds in any one wood, a man shooting pigeons will not create too much havoc. Dogs can of course be barred, but if it is thought that there are too many pheasants about, in many woods a dog may not do any harm. Although it was probably being extra cautious, I did not allow dogs when pigeon shooting, at any time or place.

Perhaps a word of caution would not be out of place. It often happens that, once pigeon shooting starts, after the game shooting ends, there will be guns out over a very large area. With the guns in the main coverts, many pheasants will remain out in the fields until almost dark and quite a few of them will go to roost in hedgerows, trees and any nearby spinney. These spinneys are danger points, not from a gun after pigeons, but I have known poachers slip in as the light fails, shoot a couple of pheasants and be gone. These men aren't worried about the end of the shooting season, a pheasant is a pheasant at any time to them. If there is this possibility, it might be as well to ask your regular men to keep their ears open and report to you should they hear a shot or two in an unexpected place. A good pigeon shooter should not ramble about all over the place, but stay put in his selected spot, whether he's getting any shooting or not!

2 · FEBRUARY

WITH THE END of the shooting season upon us, many members of small syndicates tend to lose interest and leave any jobs that need to be done to one or two willing members. It would be much better if, when the shooting season is over, a rota of syndicate members was drawn up with every individual responsible for at least one visit a week, even if only to have a word with the owners or farming tenants of the land. In this way, the people living on the shoot will get to know each member of the syndicate personally, and this often creates a much more helpful attitude.

Modern methods of rearing game birds enable strong healthy birds to be released on a shoot but they are still vulnerable to some predators. Should you be lucky enough to have a shoot, be it with a rearing programme or not, which has a suitable environment for game to rear a 'wild' brood, it is most essential to pay a lot of attention to the control of predators.

In the last chapter, pigeon shooting was dealt with, but there is no reason why, if you have a wood in which carrion-crows roost for the night, you shouldn't have a go at this black voracious bird. These cunning black birds are quite easy to shoot coming in to roost. They differ in a few ways from pigeon but, as a rule, are much later in coming to their nightly roost.

Should you consider this way of reducing the crow population, it is advisable to ensure that the birds are using the roost regularly. This is

The 'black gang' – magpie and crow.

where an evening visit of a syndicate member will prove useful. Once the regular use has been established, plans must be laid for the evening shoot. It would not be a bad idea if all members and even a few friends were to be present on the evening chosen. Now, there are evenings and evenings but long experience proves that the best time of all is when there is a good moon, with just a small amount of wind. The wind usually brings the crows in at a lower altitude! Using a similar system to pigeon shooting, often a large number of carrion crows can be killed in one night. They will continue to be airborne for some time after actual nightfall, so the guns must be patient and not shoot at birds that are a bit on the high side. Eventually they will drop into the trees; as the operation is designed to reduce the numbers, there is no reason why they should not actually be shot out of the trees. Not very sporting perhaps, but very helpful in keeping these villains down to acceptable numbers. Some will say it is not worth the cost of the cartridges, but if you remember how fond of eggs and game-bird chicks the crows are, it will put a bit of a different light on the matter.

Should your shoot be in hill country, which usually means sheep country, and crows are roosting off your shoot, it could be worth while enquiring from the owner of the wood involved what his views are on these black pests. Crows have been known to peck the eyes out of newly-born lambs, so many shepherds detest them. If it is possible to get permission to enter this off-shoot wood with a crow shoot in mind, you will certainly be helping to control the number of crows likely to nest on your patch and help the farmers at the same time. Who knows, this may even lead to permission to shoot over another farm, or at least have another source of information about movements of game and trespass or poaching.

Magpies can be reduced in numbers in a similar way to crows but, as a rule, these really delightful birds have a different roosting pattern. They normally prefer a softwood plantation and come to roost often earlier than the black 'uns, usually in small groups which gather in January and February when pairing takes place.

These two members of the corvine family are pretty numerous everywhere, so have no qualms about reducing the numbers a little. In areas where no shooting takes place, they are plentiful and breed with immunity, so should you kill every crow and magpie on your patch, the vacuum will soon be filled from surrounding areas. This is only February; a lot more can be done in the coming month or so and this will be described later.

Hopefully you have a syndicate member visiting the shoot every week as suggested earlier. It is obvious that, in an hour or so's visit, not much can be done about dealing with other predators on the shoot but once again, in sheep country, it is possible to help the shoot and the shepherd at the same time. On many of these hill shoots, no hunting takes place. Any foxes that arrive are best dealt with as soon as possible. Maybe the member of the shoot visiting lacks the knowledge or expertise to detect the presence of Reynard, but most of the shepherds and farmers are good at this and, no doubt, would welcome the assistance of any syndicate members who can be present at a drive or two. With lambing taking place early in the New Year, foxes are far from welcome in these places.

In these days, with few rabbits in most places, much less in the way of ground predators roams the countryside, but even one bitch stoat, or a rat or two, can kill a lot of game chicks. Maybe on your shoot if you haven't done so already it would be worth while placing one or two tunnel traps in suitable places: at the base of a hedge, or a gap in a stone wall, or alongside a stream. If this is done, you must ensure that the farmer, shepherd or other person is willing to look at these traps every day. Probably, if the traps are situated close to a farm or sheep pen, they will be quite willing to do this to your mutual advantage.

*   *   *

Once again the game-shooting season seems to pass faster every year. It doesn't seem long since the pheasants were laying, and it won't be long before they are doing it again. If you are keeping hen birds penned to produce eggs for you, this is the month to make sure you have enough caught up for your requirements. It is always a good idea to have one or two spare cock birds. As is well known, cock pheasants will fight to the death and, if this happens, you may find yourself short of a cock bird. Seven or eight hens per cock is about right; should the number be much higher there is always a risk of lower fertility in the eggs. If you have a spare male bird to replace any unforeseen losses, the high fertility hoped for should be maintained. If possible, keep these reserve birds or bird penned on their own, thus avoiding any fighting as the breeding season approaches.

You will find it most difficult to catch a pheasant on the shoot in April or May. By then they are well dispersed and more or less independent of any food hopper. Many times, over the years, people have come to me in search of a cock pheasant during the laying season and, because I had the required facilities to keep a number of birds penned on their own, they were usually lucky.

Although the game-shooting season is over, there is always a chance of the pigeons and crows coming into roost. One season recently I noticed that there appeared to be a great increase in the grey squirrel. Large numbers were to be seen under and around the horse-chestnut and oak trees, busy either eating the conkers and acorns or taking them away to be hidden in the winter store. They seem to forget the location of these stores so, in severe weather, not only the squirrels but mice and other rodents benefit from them.

People with rough shoot may think a grey squirrel is not worth using a cartridge on but 'tree rats', as many countrymen call them, can do quite a lot of damage to game birds, as well as to many other smaller birds during the nesting season. They will eat eggs and small fledglings. I once saw a squirrel kill a 6-week-old pheasant poult. Admittedly, the poult was cornered against some wire netting but nevertheless the squirrel wasn't many seconds in killing the unfortunate bird.

So why not have a go at the squirrels if you have a fair number in the woods on your shoot. There are several ways of dealing with the grey but, sporting wise, the best way is to shoot them. It is the most effective way of reducing the numbers. Like rats, you'll never get the last one!

You do need a bit of equipment to do the job properly, as well as a gun and a good supply of cartridges. The essential item is a set of poles which are made especially for the job. Usually in 5 foot sections and sets of ten, they are ideal for poking out the squirrel dreys, for this is what you have to do. These sets of poles are rather expensive to buy, but many agricultural colleges have them and will lend them out or hire them to *bona fide* people.

The squirrel dreys are usually most numerous in hardwood woods. It is rather useless looking for them in a large standing of softwoods. Let's assume you have a medium-sized wood of oak, ash and maybe beech and lime. You have seen a number of squirrels in this area and also some dreys in the forks of the trees, just the place to have a go poking the dreys out. I have found that the best way is to start at one end of the wood and walk roughly in line down the wood to the other end. Whilst doing this, you can look out for the dreys and also for any squirrels that may be out of their residence. Naturally you can have a shot at any that are within range, but often they start to make for their drey as soon as you enter the wood. Now, the one advantage of walking the wood 'blank' is to ensure that as many as possible of the tree rats are in their dreys. Reaching the far end of the wood, you can then start to poke the dreys out with the poles. It is best to get right against the trunk of the tree and slide the poles up the tree as you join section to section, until the drey is reached. Give the bottom of the drey a gentle tap and hopefully an occupant will emerge! Should one do so, it will present a most difficult target to the waiting guns. If possible, it is advisable to work in a gang of at least four whilst the poles are being joined and you are gradually getting closer to the drey, as sometimes a squirrel will hear the noise and decide to leave home. With two doing the poking and another two with guns at the ready, this early leaver has less chance to escape.

It is quite hard work using the poles for long; the arms and shoulders start to ache. With four in the party, working two and two about, everyone has a share of the work and the sport. Don't be disheartened if there isn't a squirrel in every drey, and don't leave any that look neglected; that's often the one the squirrels are in! Why not try a day at it if you can borrow or hire the poles, and why not combine it with shooting the pigeons coming in to roost. Four hours after squirrels, a leisurely lunch, and an hour or so waiting for pigeons, what a lovely way to spend a Saturday!

Many amusing, and for that matter annoying, things happen during the shooting season, but I came across a photograph the other day, which reminded me of an incident that happened quite a number of years ago now. Like most branches of farming, pig farming has changed a lot over the years, but this incident happened when the pigs, sows and boars, were often fastened in a large run, maybe half an acre in size.

It was during the second drive on the first shoot, a large area of kale being driven towards the home cover, with farm buildings in front of the guns and a large pen of pigs to the right of the end gun on peg six. (There were two back guns.) The pheasants were being flushed nice and steady out of the kale and spreading themselves evenly over the guns, which were dealing with them quite well, despite the fact that they were good, high, fast-flying birds. Naturally the keeper was delighted to see things going so well and was looking forward to a good bag from this one stand alone. It so happened that the gun on peg number six was a well-known gentleman who shall be nameless, and an excellent shot. He always instructed the loader to count the number of birds he killed. (An almost impossible task when the birds are coming fast and furious.) However, at the end of the drive, when picking up started, it was necessary to go into the pig run to gather the birds. The nameless gentleman knew he had quite a number in that direction and the loader, when asked, said 'Twenty-three sir' (probably guessing). The man picking up had only found a couple, when he had to make a hasty retreat, chased by an angry boar! This boar had part of a pheasant hanging from its jowl. Attempts were made to drive the boar away without success and, after a number of sows were seen happily eating plump warm pheasants, the task was abandoned. Nobody knows how many pheasants were lost that way, in the 'teens probably. However, the bag on that one drive I remember was 187 – and the pigs were happy!

*   *   *

This is the month when the shooting man reflects. He reflects on what has been, might have been, or should have been. But, by and large, sportsmen are optimistic types and, despite the inevitable disappointments, always hope that next time it will be better.

There are several ways of looking at the season's shooting. Some judge it by the number of head killed, some by the number of days shooting and some by the quality of sport. I personally have judged the many shooting seasons I have seen, first and foremost, by the quality of the sport, though it is also helpful if a reasonable bag has been obtained. I can see little pleasure in large bags made up for the most part of low-flying, even immature, birds.

Knowing full well that the only way many folk can get their (pheasant) shooting is by making the shoot give pretty good returns, it still seems a shame that low unsporting shots have to be taken to produce a good bag for sale. I suppose the shoots that have to be run like this are judged on the number of head produced.

Very often this sort of situation puts a lot of pressure on a keeper (if one is employed) and is really rather unfair on a man whose object is to provide good sport. I can remember one occasion when a gun was sent home for shooting birds that were too low. Perhaps I come from the old school that finds it hard to change to what seems to be coming increasingly more common, the modern way of running a small shoot!

The disappointments of a day's shooting are soon forgotten.

Perhaps there weren't as many birds in a certain wood as had been expected; perhaps too many broke away from the guns or perhaps it was only the weather that was foul. It is rare for the weather to stop a day's organised shoot. Rain and snow seldom stop the hardy sportsman but fog is a different matter. Flying birds are not so easily seen and it can be dangerous for all involved, especially should any of the beaters be employed as stops. In any case, one won't be able to see the real high flyers, the true sporting shot.

Reflect on the season; see if anything can be done to improve the quality of the sport; aim at good high birds, even if the bag should be reduced a bit. I remember one noble Lord saying to me once 'I only killed six birds at that rise, every one high and flying fast, worth sixty low ones', perhaps a bit of an exaggeration, but he surely preferred the sporting shots, and so should we all.

February is the month in which you should make plans for next season if you haven't already done so. There is still plenty of time to catch stock birds. Give them a week or so after the last shoot and, when they have settled down, you should have no problems.

Tunnel traps are often neglected during the shooting season. Now is a good time to renovate them and maybe change the site if little has been caught. Stoats in particular will soon be running. If you have seen a bitch stoat really busy amongst young pheasant, or for that matter any young game birds, you will be anxious to ensure there are as few as possible on your patch. Should you catch a bitch stoat in a tunnel trap at this time of the year, it is a good idea to bury it, if possible on top of the tunnel or as close to the tunnel as you can. Any dog stoats in the area are sure to scent the bitch and you stand a good chance of catching one, or even two or three. Weasels aren't quite so devastating where young game is concerned, but I have actually seen one kill a full-grown hare, so too many around a game preserve are not a good thing. Stoats, weasels and, of course, the rats can be controlled quite well with a number of tunnel traps in the right sites.

Fox hunting and many country sports are under pressure from the anti-blood-sports groups but, by and large, most shooting men welcome the hunt over their land. There has to be goodwill on both sides, for a pack of hounds running through a rather isolated covert in

Stoat caught in a tunnel trap (roof removed).

early November, before any shooting has taken place, can cause havoc. Too much disturbance and the game will seek pastures new, and many of them never return. By co-operation with the hunt, this can be avoided, even if it means that no hunting takes place in this area until almost the end of the shooting season. A lot of hunting people shoot as well, so in most cases will appreciate the problems caused. To hunt a pack of foxhounds, goodwill is essential, so the Master will usually co-operate.

This means that by February, there will be areas which have not seen the hounds since cubbing started. The hunt will appreciate assistance from the shooting men, for it is to their advantage to control the fox population. Most hunts have organised 'earth stoppers' who go out at night to 'stop' all fox earths on the area to be hunted the following day, but they are always glad of volunteers, and who better for this task than the man or men who shoot the area.

Writing about earth stopping brings to mind a true story about one such man. 'Togo' had been stopping this particular area for many years and knew all the earths and almost each individual fox around.

This time the hounds were meeting because of a large number of complaints of a fox killing chickens, and even lambs.

Just before the hounds moved off, the Master asked Togo where this fox was likely to be and, of course, Togo knew. The hounds made this wood their first 'draw' and, sure enough, out goes Reynard, but not for far. He soon slipped to ground in a large rabbit hole (it was probably a vixen). The Master then decided, in view of the complaints, to have the fox dug out. There did not seem to be any terriers available that day, so Togo was asked to start digging. It was heavy going, being solid clay in that spot. After an hour or two hard graft, poor old Togo had not progressed far; the hole turned out to be about 4 feet deep. When a mounted follower of hounds came to see what progress had been made, Togo had only travelled about 3 yards! Looking down at Togo, the chap said 'Any luck?', and of course the reply was negative, whereupon the man on the horse said 'You ought to have a JCB for that'. Togo replied 'No thank ee sir, I don't want no decorations, I does this for love'. I don't think that fox was ever accounted for. Maybe one killed by the pack during the course of the day was the guilty one, for no further complaints of chickens or lambs being killed were heard that season.

*   *   *

The end of the game-shooting season seems to come round quicker every year; a sign, they say, of age. Hoping that the past few months have been most enjoyable and productive, it is time to take stock of the situation and see if any improvements are possible for the next shooting season. No doubt many new ideas have been tried out over the last few months and quite a few lessons learnt but, with no shooting expeditions to plan, there is now time to evaluate any new developments. Plans must also be made if it is intended to do any rearing. It is never too early in the year to order your requirements in this respect.

Just because the shooting has finished, don't stop feeding any game left on your patch. There may only be a comparatively small number of birds left, but so often the most severe weather is during the month of February. Natural feed is scarce and, if you fail to feed your birds, they will soon find their way to another source of food, more than likely over your boundary! A couple of feed hoppers would only need topping up now and again and that is well worth the effort. The professional gamekeeper would often feed his birds by hand until well into April, in fact until there were no longer any coming to feed. I can assure you they didn't do that just for the fun of it! This feeding by hand also gave the gamekeeper the opportunity to observe any predators on his beat and enabled him to deal with them before they could do much damage.

There is no doubt that a weasel is partial to game chicks when the opportunity is there. I have written a lot about predators over the last year or so, but I do not apologise for doing so again. Many people, even shooting men, do not realise what a difference it makes if these enemies of game are kept under reasonable control. Don't forget the crows and magpies either!

In these days of conservation, some folks would like to see all wildlife protected, but it makes one wonder what the countryside would be like in, say 20 years if this happened. There has to be a reasonable balance and, in my long years as a gamekeeper, I have

Hen pheasant feeding at hopper.

observed that all wildlife prospers on a large estate that is well keepered; in fact the bird watchers love to have permission to visit such places.

Quite a lot of changes take place this month; it is the time when gamekeepers often change their situation and when, with a bit of luck, a lad will get his first opportunity to enter the profession. It was often the case that a gamekeeper's son would follow in his father's footsteps, and such a lad would have a head start, having lived 'game' all his life. Today it seems to me, many town and urban lads are keen to become gamekeepers. I am often asked by their parents the best way to go about it. As with so many jobs these days, the opportunities are just not there. It does help if, during the summer holidays and at weekends, an interested lad helps a keeper and gets to know some of the jobs entailed. A lad must be keen and not expect to be carrying a gun around all day as some expect to do! A foothold in the job does not mean he will have a chance to climb the ladder, but it does and must give him a better chance. Most keepers are pretty good at assessing potential and a word in the right place can often give a good lad the chance he needs.

Not only do keepers change their situation at this time of the year, but often syndicates give up and another 'gang' of shooters take over. Rough shooting is not so often on the market, but the odd area does become available now and again. There are many things to be considered should you have the opportunity to be involved in either. Take a syndicate shoot; when all the members decide not to carry on, there must be a good reason, one that any interested party may not easily be able to find out. Perhaps the cost of running the shoot has gone too high for the purses of the members. Should this be so, there must be a reason for it. Questions must be asked. Have the birds been reared on site? Have they been brought in as poults or are wild birds only relied on? If the chicks have been hatched and reared by a keeper, has there been unnecessary expense? The Game Conservancy can supply figures that will give a good guide to this. Poults that are bought in are not cheap, but even so they can be advantageous, particularly if wild birds do well on that shoot, for it gives a keeper the time to look after the nesting birds. When it comes to relying on wild birds alone, things become a bit dodgy, for it is very difficult to know what stock has been left after the shooting season. The number of predators can also affect the potential and, of course, the attitude of the farmers can be crucial.

The keeper on a syndicate, or for that matter any shoot, has to be the key man and, in most cases, when syndicated shooting is changing hands, part of the deal is that the keeper remains. It is essential that a good relationship is maintained between those who pay and the keeper. Most keepers like a pretty free hand, for they are nearly always working on their own most of the time. It is essential to make it very clear how far the key man can go in spending the syndicate's money, but it is advisable to give a free hand as far as the type and supplier of feed is concerned. I have known a keeper blame the feed after a poor rearing season when the supplier has been forced on him by the man in charge of the shoot. A poor excuse maybe but, if he has a free hand in this respect, at least it's one thing he can't blame! It is also essential, in my opinion, that only one member of the shoot gives instructions to the keeper. Nothing can be more confusing than conflicting orders. When matters concerning the winter's sport are being discussed at a pre-season meeting of the syndicate, it is advisable for the keeper to attend. It gives him a good opportunity to judge what is planned and what is required of him. He will probably come up with a good idea or two, for he probably has far greater knowledge of the area and movement of birds than anyone else.

The rough shoot is a different kettle of fish than a shoot where a keeper is employed, but nevertheless a lot of information is needed before paying good money for the right to shoot over any area. The type of country is important, for there will be little sport on an area devoid of cover, except maybe pigeon shooting over crops. A nice little wood or two is a great advantage and some water, whether it be lake, pond or river, gives the area at least some potential. It is essential to know, once again, the attitude of the farmer or farmers. A farmer who is keen on shooting is not always the best man to deal with, for so often he will want his share of what you are paying for! A good farmer will be delighted if you hope to turn a few pheasants or ducks down and probably will help with the feeding of same. Should you decide that such a shoot is a viable one, make sure you have a proper agreement with the farmer or farmers. I shall not go into this, for each case can be so different, but an agreement in writing signed by both parties may prove invaluable in the future.

3 · MARCH

THIS IS THE MONTH when small unkeepered syndicate shoots should take stock of the past season's successes and failures and make plans for the next shooting season, which somehow will be very soon upon us.

It can be very helpful if, say, three members of the syndicate, preferably those with the most shooting experience spend a day on the shoot and very carefully go over at least the most important drives. With plenty of time, and without the excitement of a shooting day, it is often possible to find ways of improving even an already 'good' rise.

Cover is a very important factor in determining where the pheasants are going to be when the wood is driven – it is from here that the birds will be put into the air. Maybe in one particular drive the pheasants tend to break back over the left-hand gun, who is often the only one to get any shooting. If the bulk of the ground cover is on the right-hand side or corner of the wood (from the beaters' point), the birds are almost sure to break over the left-hand gun or guns. By taking plenty of time and assessing all the possibilities very carefully, there is often a chance of improving the situation. It would probably not be advisable to clear existing low-growing cover, but it may be possible to increase the 'hide' for the birds, either centrally or on the left flank. That should improve the particular drive, with some of the birds going over every gun, which no doubt would be appreciated.

Ground cover need not necessarily be planted. Sometimes a thorn bush can be 'laid', i.e. cut half or two-thirds through and pushed over. If this is done during March, it is almost certain that nettles or rough grass will grow through and be held up by the bush – ready-made cover with a stroke or two of an axe! No thorn bushes? Not to worry, any bushy material may be put in the position required with the same effect. You may say 'Ah! but there are no nettles or grass where the cover is wanted', but of course there is no reason why grass seed should not be scattered where you want the cover. Cocksfoot is probably the best seed to use and, hopefully, you can purchase this particular type. If not, rye grass is not too bad. At a push, barley can be sown, but this does not usually provide the same amount of cover as the grasses. The straw tends to rot and the birds will pull at the grain which will all reduce the amount of cover. If you have to sow any of the grasses or grain, it is much better to do this before the thorns are laid or other cut bushes put into position. Raking the seed in and then putting the bushes on will reduce the amount small birds will take.

Very little labour is required to do what has been described and sometimes it will improve a particular rise beyond all recognition. Don't try and do too much in any one season, but there is no doubt a few small things can improve the sport no end. Just a word of caution. Make sure the owner of the woods has no objection to any improvements you try to make. He shouldn't have, but make sure. It would even help if the owner could be present when you were deciding what to do.

Now, improving the sporting possibilities of a shoot is not much good without game to shoot! Most small shoots rear a few pheasants these days. The cost of doing this is the factor that more or less controls the number of birds reared. If hen pheasants have been caught up or kept back from last year's rearing for egg production, now is the time to start ensuring that egg production will be good and fertility high. There are several ways of penning the birds, which obviously will depend upon the material and ground available. It is probably best if the stock birds can be moved fairly regularly to clean ground, which means a movable pen. This needs quite a lot of ground and, more than likely, several pens which, being moved frequently, need to be very well constructed. The normal number of birds to this type of pen is eight hens and one cockbird. If treated correctly, each hen bird should produce approximately 40 eggs between April and early June. A fixed pen is probably more suitable and the ideal size for nine birds is 20 feet by 10 feet. Of course, these fixed pens get rather muddy during wet weather, but it is not advisable to use straw to keep it clean. Straw can carry a number of viral and other diseases, so reasonably fine gravel or sand is preferable.

Feeding is most important. It never pays to try and do it on the cheap. After many years of experience, the following has been found the best method to adopt. Assuming the pheasants have been put in their laying pens by mid-February, they should be fed on a good-quality wheat once a day, or *ad lib* in a hopper until 1 March, when the feed should be changed to a breeder pellet, and a small handful of wheat per pen each evening. Some will say this is expensive and that April is soon enough to use breeder pellets. Fair enough if you don't propose to hatch pheasants too early, but by using these pellets one month before you put eggs to hatch, it will be found that the fertility

Young assistant keeper feeds birds in laying pen. Note his correct dress. He whistles to accustom the birds to him.

will be much higher than eggs from birds fed by cheaper methods. Don't forget that all game birds also need oyster shell. These days, it is possible to get a ready-mixed material which provides all the laying birds need in this respect. Be generous with grit; even when badly in need of it, game birds can be very particular. Even with what appears to be plenty in the pen, they may not have exactly what they need. Give a good handful to each pen once a week and all will be well.

Many people have trouble with birds eating the eggs. This is practically universal these days and is undoubtedly due to the higher protein content of the modern compounded feeds. Pre-war there was, as far as can be recalled, none of this trouble. The cure is simple enough. Get some plastic 'specs', which are quite cheap, and fit the birds with them before putting them in their laying quarters. The bits used to prevent feather pecking are not really suitable for this purpose, so use the specs obtainable from any firm which deals in game-rearing equipment.

*   *   *

Dealing with the grey squirrel was one of the topics discussed in the last chapter and, hopefully, you had some sport poking out the dreys. It is often surprising how many of the little grey beasties will come out of one drey, but no matter how many you are successful in shooting, there will always be quite a lot left to breed.

This applies to all predators of game so it is essential to keep up a relentless war against the worst offenders. (Squirrels don't come into this category, but there are enough without.) A few tunnel traps would be well worth while, so long as a reliable person was available to 'look' for them every day. Very often, asking someone to co-operate and keep their eyes on the tunnels can generate an interest in the shooting and, if you do this, it is a great help. It is remarkable how many people help out like this and are, in fact, often the mainstay of a shoot where those holding the sporting rights live some distance away.

Back to the tunnel traps. If you have not done so already, these should be renovated. Even a really well-built one can become dilapidated after catching, say, a rabbit or two. Sometimes a 'tunnel' despite being in what appears to be an attractive spot, has very little

Resetting a Fenn trap.

success. Now is a good time to look for another place. It is very difficult to suggest a suitable spot. Much depends on the terrain but, by and large, if you use any hole, be it in a stone wall, an old tree or a drain, success is more likely. A hedge that runs down to a stream is often a very good spot as it will pick up stoats, weasels and rats, either going for, or coming back from a drink.

On a small rough spot or unkeepered syndicate, it is not a good idea to set too many tunnel traps. You have to rely on a willing helper to look at them and they should be looked at every day. The modern so-called humane Fenn trap is not always so humane as it is supposed to be, so, to save any suffering, the tunnels must be 'looked' every day. The professional gamekeeper will often look at the tunnel traps twice a day and, when other duties are more pressing, will spring the traps for a week or two. An old-timer once said to the writer many years ago 'Look after the tunnels, lad, they are working when you're not', but really there isn't much time when a keeper isn't working!

March means it won't be long before the pheasants start to lay. Have you fed the stock birds properly? Breeder pellets are suggested from 1

March. This is a practice that can't be improved upon. It may be difficult to obtain these pellets in small quantities, but make every effort to do so. In the end it will pay good dividends. You may know friends who are also producing a few eggs from their own stock. If you can co-operate most food game merchants will deliver 10 hundred-weight or so. Don't, if you can avoid it, feed your pheasant laying pellets, although it may seem the right thing. It is fertile, hatchable eggs you want and the laying pellets are designed to produce the maximum number of eggs not good quality 'hatching' eggs. It may appear to be rather splitting hairs but you can rest assured that the difference will show when hatching time comes. So don't forget, breeder pellets, or turkey breeder pellets if you can't get those designed for game, though there is actually little difference. Start feeding them to your birds not much later than 1 March.

Knowing full well that many readers try to operate their shoot as cheaply as possible, often of necessity, it still must be emphasised that, as far as game birds are concerned, it is often cheaper in the long run to use the best. Don't economise on the feed, even if the equipment has to be a bit ramshackle!

The spring is fast approaching and the welcome song of the numerous birds that visit our shores to breed will be heard. Unfortunately, there do not seem to be as many or as many species as when I was a youth but nevertheless a chorus of most delightful ditties can be heard if you are in the right place at the right time.

In the county where I live, the chiff-chaff is nearly always the first of our summer visitors to be heard, often in the first week of March, soon to be followed by the willow wren, garden warbler and 'Peggy' whitethroat. Really, our summer countryside would be rather dull without these and other migrants that honour us with their presence during the nesting season.

There must be many reasons why we do not have so many visitors as in the past, probably as many reasons as the people who propound them. There cannot be much doubt that most, if not all, of the causes of the reduction are the actions of Man.

From the netting of small birds on their migrant passage in foreign countries, to the use of sprays and fertilisers in Britain, all play havoc with our feathered friends. Very few birds do damage to farm crops, in fact most of them serve a very useful purpose. (We won't go into the habits and greed of pigeons!) There can be little doubt that the reduction of bird life must, at sometime and somewhere, upset the delicate balance of nature.

I can no longer hear from my bedroom window the shrill song of the grasshopper warbler, so often heard in April not many years ago. Last year, despite a diligent search, only two bird's nests could be found in the large garden. A few years ago, it was not at all unusual for there to be seven or eight nests in the same place. These would include goldfinch, chaffinch, hedge sparrow and, of course, thrush and blackbird. There were four or five different species, against the lonely two pairs of blackbirds last season. May this year be an improvement.

I make no apologies for these few words about bird life. All true countrymen and shooting people should be interested in and, wherever possible, preserve this heritage of ours. There are few things more entrancing than listening to the dawn chorus on a lovely warm and still early spring morning. Fewer people are about at that time of day than used to be, so maybe the loss of so many of our early songsters is not appreciated as it should be.

It is said that larger tractors, larger machines, larger fields and large amounts of fertilisers and sprays are essential to make farming a viable proposition today. I am not aware of the financial side of farming, but there must come a time when a limit will be reached. Perhaps when that day comes it will be to the advantage of wildlife.

There does seem to be a growing realisation amongst many of the farming community that much is being lost. Some are paying a lot more attention to making any otherwise 'waste' areas of land into suitable habitat for wildlife of all sorts. This can only be to everyone's advantage and hopefully will be extended to much larger areas than at present. It may be a coincidence but most farmers I know who are showing an interest in this conservation are also keen shooting men. We must hope the good work is kept up!

*   *   *

A greater interest in the conservation and preservation of our rural heritage must provide greater possibilities for wild game birds. In the last 12 months there seems to have been much less uprooting of hedges and quite a lot of planting in odd corners. This can only help the stock of wild birds – not only game birds, but all birds.

Sometimes the planting of awkward pieces of ground is not done to the best advantage. If the area is large enough, some ground cover is needed as well as a tree or two. A few shrubs which produce berries are very suitable and, failing that, a patch of briars (blackberry) can be most useful. The object must be to provide some not too dense cover and, wherever possible, something that game birds like to feed on. Rough grass or even the common nettle is better than nothing. The stinging nettle, although not particularly popular with game birds, is host to numerous insects of which game birds are very fond.

In a wood full of released poults, I have noticed a patch of nettles stripped of foliage as high as the birds can jump. Observation proved that the pheasants were really after the insects on the nettles but at the same time were eating some of the leaves. Many of the undersides of the leaves were covered in small insects, but the leaves which the poults had not touched were clear. It must be assumed that, as the insects were so small, the birds devoured leaf and all.

Phil Drabble, the eminent naturalist and broadcaster, maintains an area of 90 acres around his home as a natural reserve. He finds that the population of wildlife, after it has bred, helps to re-stock the surrounding coutryside. Even then there must be suitable habitat where the young stock can go. Most shoots have woodlands that are, in effect, a nature reserve. The planting of odd areas creates somewhere for this young stock to go. It is in the interest of all shooting and sporting men to do their best to preserve our wildlife, despite the fact that game birds have a number of enemies! In over 50 years looking after game and dealing with what they call 'predators' today (we called them 'vermin'; still rat catchers are 'rodent operatives' now), there seems to be more of the crow tribe about and no shortage of sparrow hawks, not to mention foxes!

I think Phil Drabble's endeavours to provide a sanctuary for wild-life has proved most successful. It would be a great advantage to our wildlife if there were many more areas throughout our countryside that were treated with the loving care that Phil bestows on his patch. A large sporting estate does to a lesser degree what Phil does, for in the production of game it is essential that there is the minimum of disturbance and reasonable control of predators. Of course on 900 acres it is not possible to bestow the same attention as on Phil's 90 but, with diligence and the co-operation of the farming community, it is surprising what can be achieved.

Even small shoots having the shooting over several farms can achieve quite a lot. The planting of small areas will often get the blessing of the farm owners and be beneficial to all concerned. It seems to me essential these days to be able to point to things which are to the advantage of the wildlife and are not the 'target' of the shooting man. There is certainly a fair amount of opposition to so called 'blood sports'. Even fishing for pleasure is now under fire, though no mention has been made, as far as I know, of fishing commercially. How much further do these 'antis' intend to go? Perhaps we shall all end up vegetarians! Maybe even then there would be some bright spark who would claim that a lettuce suffers when it is cut for use in a salad!

The areas most frequented by bird watchers are the sporting estates. That seems to me to prove that wildlife has more peace and a better chance of breeding on such places. The reader may think the foregoing has not a lot to do with his 'patch' but I think it should be emphasised that, with what appears to be mounting, or at least well-publicised, opposition to all country sports, everyone should play his part, no matter how small, to offset the sometimes childish capers of the 'antis'.

An incident from the past has just come to mind which may be of interest. It happened many years ago when it was not illegal to set baited traps for vermin, a procedure most keepers followed in those days. A number of bird watchers had permission to visit a particular estate in the furtherance of their hobby, and did so with the co-operation of the gamekeepers. This had gone on for many years until a person who did not have permission to be there reported anonymously

---

A crow trap, with ladder-type slit entrance. Demonstrated at the 1967 Game Fair.

to the Royal Society for the Protection of Birds that a carrion crow had been seen in a baited trap. The secretary of that society contacted the estate owner, who quite naturally refused to take any action, but promised to do something if the person complaining approached him personally. This did not happen so the net result was that the regular bird watchers were banned from the estate. This ban lasted for more than 2 years, when once again permission was given to a selected number, who were understandably keen to retain their privilege and always reported to the keepers the presence of any strangers on the estate!

March is the month when many birds start nesting and amongst the earliest are the mallard, something I cannot really understand. Young wild duckling need insects to survive and eggs laid in early March will be hatching in April, when any great quantity of insects is most unlikely. Many times I have seen a good brood of ducklings in mid-April and observed that a week later the poor old duck is left with maybe a couple, almost certainly due to a lack of those high-protein insects so essential for the first 10 days or so. Sometimes March can be a comparatively mild month and quite a lot of mallard will start to nest (I once found sitting mallard on 12 January). If you know of a number of nests on your shoot in March, it may well be worth while collecting the eggs when a nest contains seven or so (by an authorised person until 31 March) and hatching these either under broody hens (a bit scarce in March) or in an incubator.

Duckling are easy to rear, needing only a small amount of heat after the first week. A 100 watt bulb hung over a largish box is enough to rear quite a lot of ducklings. They must be fed a high protein feed, such as turkey or pheasant crumbs, for 10 days or so. The water provided must be shallow or the youngsters, lacking the oil from the mother duck, will drown. After 10 days, less heat is needed and a cheaper form of food is all that is required. As they grow, a grass run should be available, with ready access to minimal heat. They make a bit of a mess when they are older, but you must think of the sport they will provide later on!

By taking these early eggs there is a much better chance that the duck will be more successful with a later brood, hatching when feed is more readily available. In March, ground cover is pretty sparse so, by the time the duck nests again, and it is 100 per cent certain that she will, more cover will be there to conceal the eggs – crows love them!

*　　*　　*

There is a lot that can and should be done on any shoot, large or small. It won't be long before the game birds are laying and, to get good fertile eggs, the stock birds must have the right food at least a month before egg production. Grit is essential too, for birds that are penned may find it difficult to get enough. A mixture of oyster shell and flint grit once a week, even if there is still some lying in the pens, is a good policy and not expensive either. Care must be taken to ensure the hen birds do not become too fat. If this occurs, problems may ensue once laying commences. An egg-bound bird is a 'dead' loss, so feed the stock birds on breeder pellets, and maybe a few grains of wheat in the evening. Make sure you are feeding breeder and not laying pellets. It is much better to have fewer eggs with high fertility so you won't be wasting incubator space on clear eggs!

Many syndicates and even large shoots buy in their birds as poults. If this is the case, time is running out to order them. There seems to be a tendency to buy poults from the later hatches, mainly for economy reasons. Unless you have the order in at the game farm early, you may have to take the earlier birds, and thus push up your feed bills and probably lose more from that unpredictable habit of game birds – straying!

Before the leaves are on the trees is a good time to find out where the carrion crows are setting up home. The carrion is a pretty early nester. From about the middle of March, it should be possible to spot that often untidy-looking bundle of twigs, whether in the topmost branches of a lonesome tree or packed tight in the fork of a hedgerow oak. Knowing where the nest is makes it that much easier to deal with this black predator once the bird starts to incubate. It is not easy to approach the nest without putting the sitting bird off. Many times the crafty corvid will slip out on the far side unseen by the approaching gunman. If two men approach the nest and one takes up a hidden position within range of the nest, it is rarely more than 20 minutes

before the unsuspecting bird returns. It appears that the black devil can't count up to two, so that 20 minutes can be well spent!

Magpies, so numerous these days, are a different kettle of fish. They don't nest so early but it is almost certain that if you spot an old domed nest of the 'pie' in March, and it isn't occupied in April, there will be another one very close by that is. The same applies to a crow's nest, for in many cases an old nest is renovated – but not by the original occupants if you have been around the year before! A magpie is just the opposite to a carrion crow as regards approaching the nest; even a good thumping on the base of the tree or bush (for magpies love thick hawthorn bushes) will often fail to disturb the occupant. Should the bird decide to leave home, it almost certainly will only provide you with a 'snap' shot, and a difficult one at that. In most cases, the best way to deal with the black-and-white bird is to shoot into the nest but, on doing so, endeavour to aim at a point just below the halfway point. The wily bird will be just below the rim of the actual nest, which is quite substantial, being made of sticks reinforced with mud. If your gun has a choke in it at all, use that barrel, and I would suggest a cartridge with nothing smaller than size four shot. You won't always know if the charge of shot has done its job, but in many cases it will have done; when it's boiled down I suppose it must be the lower the nest the better the chance.

I don't think I need remind anyone about how important it is that guns should be maintained in tip-top condition. After a season's shooting in all sorts of weather, and despite great care being taken with the cleaning after every outing, it is always advisable to have the weapon overhauled. Like everything these days, it is not cheap to have this done but it is money well spent, for should it let you down next shooting season, particularly if the birds are coming fast and furious, you will kick yourself. The interests of safety really demand this annual attention, for I have known a twelve bore to be discharged prematurely, when it was being loaded, fortunately without dire consequences in that particular case.

Gun cleaning and a good case of guns.

There are plenty of good gunsmiths around within reasonable reach of most shooting people and, should you be the lucky owner of a really expensive gun or guns, it would be best to send them to the makers each spring and then you would know your gun was in tip-top condition.

Living in the country, a gamekeeper in particular, often gets asked to do small 'rural' jobs. In March, moles start to be active, pushing up their hills of soil in many unwelcome places. Now moles are not all that hard to catch and most keepers have a few mole traps, and thus can deal with the underground workers when the occasion demands. As the soil warms up and the worms are nearer the surface, the moles follow them; hence the unsightly heaps of soil on an otherwise immaculate lawn. In most cases, the moles are best trapped some distance from the actual working. A run along a wall or at the base of a hedge is easily found by probing with a walking stick and, so long as the trap is set correctly (it is important that no light gets through to the run), the mole will soon be picked up and the trouble resolved.

Writing of moles reminds me of a true story which occurred a number of years ago. Between the wars many Irish labourers came to Cheshire in the spring and spent the summer doing casual jobs. One such chap was making his way through the countryside seeking work, for his cash was running low. He called on a largish house, the abode of a local squire, where he asked for something to eat in return for an hour or two's labour. The squire, being a kindly man, was only too pleased to feed the man, but was hard put to find a small job for him to do. Without much hope of the Irishman doing it, he asked if he could catch moles. 'Fur sure, Zur, now you've got the right man.' 'Well there's just one thing Paddy', says the squire, 'I shouldn't say it, but those little devils have really pestered me, so do you think you can make them suffer?' 'Be jabers I be good at that now Zur, you couldn't have got a better man.' With that, Paddy set off to deal with the offending animals.

After about an hour, there was a knock on the squire's door, Paddy calling to report his progress. The squire opened up and there was the Irishman all smiles. 'Now for sure Zur, you'll no be having any more trouble with them there moles.' 'I'm very glad to hear it Paddy', says the squire and, as he slipped him a shilling, said, 'There's just one thing, did you make them suffer?' 'For sure Zur, for sure', says Paddy. 'Well how did you manage that?' the squire inquires. 'Now indeed it was easy enough', says the Irishman. 'I buried the little varmints alive', as he made a hasty retreat. Exit the Irishman, but no doubt the squire was not pleased when the mole hills reappeared, for Paddy had spent the hour merely kicking the heaps of subsoil around!

4 · APRIL

S PRING SHOULD SOON be making its appearance and will be especially welcome if the winter has been severe. Heavy snowfalls can curtail shooting to some extent, not so much because of the low temperatures, shooting people are pretty hardy anyway, but because of the impossibility of travelling any distance in country districts. When Land Rovers can't get through, there is little chance for an ordinary car and a number of shooting forays may have had to be cancelled or postponed. Missed days can sometimes be made up in late January but, after a hard winter, there may well be more pheasants left on many shoots than in a normal year. With plenty of attention given to predators in April, this can augur well for the coming season.

One small incident happened at a large shoot on what was probably the coldest day of winter. A retired keeper, who was present with his dog to 'pick up', was an inveterate pipe smoker and, this day, was patiently waiting to carry out his allotted task. It was rather a long 'drive' so the pipe was filled to help while away the time. The smoke was rising in a blue cloud as he waited for the shooting to commence. Suddenly he could no longer draw on the pipe and the smoke dispersed. Matches were struck in an attempt to get the pipe going again. No luck. Coat and jacket were unbuttoned to get his knife to tease the baccy in the bowl. All to no avail! He was getting a bit desperate as the birds would soon be coming over and there would be no time to smoke, so he pulled the pipe apart. This soon revealed the cause of his failure to 'make smoke'; the 'goo' in the stem and the bottom of the bowl of his pipe had frozen! Now the temperature must have been low for that to freeze, half an inch from a fire! However, holding the pipe over a lighted match or two soon relieved the problem and very shortly the smoke was rising high through the trees on the still air.

Much wildlife suffers during severe weather and, hopefully, any bans on shooting wildfowl, woodcock etc. are observed. There is not much pleasure or sport in shooting poor weakened birds; they are useless for the pot and easy targets. If the weather itself takes a heavy toll bans are essential to protect as many as possible for the following year's breeding. Yes, many of them are migratory but, if they aren't here to breed, there won't be so many to visit our shores next year and, goodness knows, there are so many factors against them surviving without Man shooting them for shooting's sake. Perhaps pigeons are in a different category, but in very severe weather they soon become so thin you could almost shave yourself with the breast bone. In any case, temperatures below zero soon put paid to most green crops, so shooting them is to no avail.

The pheasants won't be laying at the moment but, under the right conditions, it is seldom later than the first day or two in April before they commence to 'shoot them out'. Wild stock are sometimes a little later, but early or late, spring does not make a lot of difference. Should it be late spring, pay particular attention to crows and magpies on the shoot. Pheasants can be a bit stupid about where they lay their eggs, often in the most exposed positions, and it doesn't take the corvids long to seek them out and devour them. An early spring means more growth and cover for the eggs, giving the pheasants a better chance, but still don't neglect to deal with the crow family.

Eggs, eggs, glorious eggs, this is where it all begins! Whether you hatch your own, as some rough and unkeepered syndicate shoots still do, or whether you send the eggs off to be 'custom-hatched', it is essential that the eggs are treated correctly from the time they are laid. It is not necessary to pick up the eggs by the minute, if the stock birds have 'specs' on they will be safe enough, but it is certainly advisable not to leave them in the open on a very hot day. The sun can be strong

Pheasants wearing 'specs' to deter them from feather-pecking.

enough even to start incubation; only very slightly of course, but an egg thus warmed will not hatch and is sometimes the reason for bad hatching results, particularly in incubators. Pick up the eggs at least twice a day if at all possible. It might only be a fad, but I prefer a wicker basket rather than a galvanised bucket. Store the eggs in egg trays at a temperature that does not fluctuate too much from 55° to 60° Fahrenheit. Now if you are having them custom-hatched, check with the hatchery when you book in whether they like the eggs washed, when new laid. They will advise you on the method and chemical to use. If you are hatching them yourself, you will find that Hydex ® is probably the best to use. This is obtainable in 2 litre containers with full instructions. Even if the weather is kind and the eggs are spotless, they must still be washed to prevent many egg borne problems.

Pheasants are mature, i.e. fully grown, at 16 weeks. Allowing a month and calling it 20 weeks, gives you an idea of when to 'set' the eggs. By knowing this, it is possible to save quite a large amount of food, labour and money. If pheasants are to be fully grown by the date of your first shoot, then 20 weeks before is the date to set your eggs!

Incubation is a well-covered subject these days but a few, maybe useful, tips from my own experiences will be found in the next chapter.

*   *   *

April is the month of promise, the month when spring really shows its hand, and the month when game birds are looking for nesting sites, if they haven't already found them.

Professional gamekeepers always like to know where the wild pheasants are nesting. Quite a lot can be done to improve their chances of hatching and rearing a reasonable brood. So much depends on the environment, which is such a changing factor these days. As a rule, pheasants choose a sunny site and, in hilly country, this usually means a bank facing south or thereabouts. I do not think it is a good idea to look for game-birds' nests deliberately, be they pheasant or partridge, unless the object is to collect eggs. No matter how careful you are, you create a disturbance by hunting for and finding nests. Perhaps 'disturbance' isn't quite the right word, but you inevitably leave a trail of evidence that can be followed by creatures that have evil intent on egg and bird. It is well known that a fox will follow a human scent and no doubt other creatures too. During a spell of snowy weather in the winter, it is not at all uncommon to see the tracks of a fox either in or following a man's tracks in the snow and, no doubt, Reynard does the same when there is no snow.

By general observation, it is possible to determine which area game birds seem to favour for nesting, and this area is well worth a little bit more attention with predator control. Carrion crows and magpies are the ones needing most attention but it is a good idea, if possible, to ensure there is a reasonable number of tunnel traps on the area, not forgetting it is essential that the traps are looked at on a regular basis. Stoats are great eaters of eggs in the spring and will hunt over a considerable area, even working in the hedges themselves for small birds' nests. Rats are a menace anywhere and at any time but, when spring comes, they desert the warm buildings and stacks of hay (not much of that about today) and straw and take to the hedgerows. Eggs are a great favourite of these rodents and it is amazing how many they can dispose of in a short time. I remember one incident many years ago

when a pen of laying pheasants received the attention of a bitch rat. While going past the pen one afternoon, I noticed six eggs in one corner; an hour later when the collecting round was made, the six eggs were no longer there. The first thought was that one of the pheasants had devoured them. Pheasants will eat their own eggs but, when they do, the shells are usually lying in the pen. This was not so in this case. Further investigation showed evidence that a rat was the culprit and the matter was soon dealt with by waiting for the rodent to appear, only to fall victim of a shot from a four ten.

An early morning visit to a shoot will often be most revealing in April; this is the best time of day to see game birds which are sitting come off the nest to feed. It is a bit early for partridge but, by late April, many pheasants will have 'gone down' on their clutch of olive eggs and, in the early morning dew, can be seen literally rushing about to get a feed and, at the same time, to get their breast feathers wet. These wet feathers help to provide the humidity required to hatch the eggs. The cock pheasant will often crow when one of his harem of hens comes off to feed, but a male pheasant is seldom in such close attendance as a male partridge and really has little to do with his several hens.

The partridge normally lays later than the pheasant and is really a much more secretive bird. A territorial bird, yes, but this does not make it any easier to find the nest. In the old days when various 'systems' were practised (the Euston was one), even some experienced gamekeepers found it difficult to find the partridge nests. The eggs are always covered by leaves or grass, according to the site, and there is rarely any evidence that the nest is there. For some unknown reason, both partridges and pheasants often favour a nesting site by the roadside. Birds nesting in such places are much more vulnerable than more sensible birds, so, particularly with pheasants, it is often best to gather the eggs and hatch them by whichever method you favour: incubator, broody hen or bantam.

There is little scent from a brooding game bird and, although dogs

---

Rats are one of the keeper's enemies: here poison is being put in their run.

seem to find them, foxes rarely take the bird until the eggs begin to chip, when there must be a very enticing smell for Reynard's ever-alert senses. A dawn visit to your shoot may well produce the sight of a fox returning to its earth or thicket after the nightly foray, and thus give you the chance either to leave it for the hounds later in the year, should you be in hunting country, or to take the required action to protect your stock of breeding birds. Oh, what a walk in the countryside at dawn in the spring is worth!

Walking the dog on what was a real spring-like day in January along the banks of the River Dee in Cheshire, I was amazed to see what was obviously a warbler busy working its ways through a leafless bed of briars. It was so busy searching the twigs for food that it took no notice of my presence. After observing it for some time, I came to the conclusion that it was either a chiff-chaff or a willow warbler. These birds are so much alike it is most difficult to tell one from the other when always on the move in a briar bush! Despite watching and waiting for some time, I did not hear the familiar call of either bird so there is only one certain thing; it was a warbler. Normally the chiff-chaff is one of the first heralds of spring here in Cheshire, usually appearing during early March, but January is most unusual.

As it had been a mild winter up to the end of January, I don't suppose it was entirely impossible for a summer visitor to be here that early but on the other hand, could this lone bird (I only saw the one) be the survivor of a very late brood from the previous year? We shall never know.

It is amazing the things that are observed in the countryside, particularly by gamekeepers, who often think nothing of what they have seen, but what a huge number of incidents must take place that go entirely unseen. Keep your eyes open, and you never know what interesting sight may befall you.

*   *   *

This is always a most interesting time of the year for all those interested in country life and April is probably the most interesting month. The summer songsters start to arrive in force but, unfortunately, not in quite the numbers they did in years gone by. The swallow and the cuckoo are probably the real signs of spring to most people, but the gamekeeper and farm worker, who spend their life on the land, see many signs before our overseas visitors arrive. The modern farm worker does not have the same chances to observe these signs as his counterpart of days gone by. Riding on tractors and using modern machinery needs a fair amount of concentration, so many of the changes are never seen. Since the end of last month many of our resident birds will have been sorting out their 'territorial rights' and searching for nesting sites. The ducks, usually mallard, are always very prominent in this respect and any Canada geese in the area make themselves known with their honking when squabbling over a nest site. Smaller birds are not so easily observed, but the gamekeeper can usually pinpoint fairly well an area where any particular birds are likely to nest.

Many years ago, before they were protected by law, it was the recognised custom to gather plover (lapwing) eggs for the table. Many country people were waiting to hear the familiar call *pee-wee-wit-wit* which was a sure sign that the birds would soon be nesting. By

Geese coming in to feed on a potato field. The inland fowler waits in a hide.

57

watching the aerial displays of the birds, it was fairly easy to pinpoint the nesting area. As a lad (that's many years ago now!), the gamekeepers on the estate had to collect the plover eggs for the annual Grand-National house party. The Grand National was always at the end of March, a bit on the early side for plovers' eggs, but in those days these birds nested on the water meadows literally in hundreds and it was possible to collect enough early eggs for the house guests to enjoy and no doubt to boast about on returning to their city homes.

Today, very few of these delightful birds nest on those very same meadows and, fortunately, the taking of eggs is against the law. Despite this law, the numbers do not seem to increase. Can modern farming methods once again be partly responsible? In the end all wildlife is controlled by the feed available and a suitable environment.

Going back to those egg-collecting days of my youth, one old keeper had a black labrador 'Tom', who was always taken on these egg-collecting expeditions. The old keeper would approach the meadow cautiously and assess the number of pairs nesting there. Then the labrador would be sent out to work the field and, having a good 'nose', would follow the line the plover had taken to its nest. If no eggs were in the scrape (and plovers make a number of false nests), Tom would carry on until he found a nest with eggs, whereupon he would 'point' like a pointer. It was usually the lad (me) who set off to collect the eggs. This grand old dog saved many a mile of walking. As the old keeper said 'Economy of effort'. Don't try and train your dog to do this; let the plovers remain in peace and hopefully increase in numbers. Perhaps future generations will hear more of that sure harbinger of spring, the plaintiff cry of the wheeling peewit.

April is a good month to deal with many of the predators that are so fond of not only game bird eggs but any eggs they can find. To see a carrion crow working a hedgerow in search of nests will bring this home forcibly. This black villain will miss nothing, often taking practically all the eggs out of every nest in that length of hedge. You can be sure that any pheasants which may have laid there will lose their eggs. I can only emphasise that all shooting people should do what they can to reduce the numbers which, by my observations, seem to be on the increase.

Don't forget the magpie either. It is quite likely that they do not take as many game-bird eggs as the crow, but they are inveterate egg eaters and could well do with being reduced in numbers. I have heard a saying about magpies 'One for sorrow, two for joy and three for a boy' and in fact many old country people would touch their head and count to twenty should they see one 'pie'. A strange custom – must have been a reason for it. I would think it was better to see one magpie than two. There is a fair chance of seeing ten or a dozen in a while with a pair of mapgies around!

It will not be long now before the *cheep, cheep* of pheasant chicks will be heard. A pleasant sound now, without the worry that the old-time keepers had. The modern brooder house, no matter what heating is used, is so much better in some respects than tramping around the coops on a rearing field. So long as all details are attended to, there is no reason why good results shouldn't be achieved. I did say 'better in some respects'; by that I was thinking of the joy of opening the coops and letting the chicks out to roam in the long insect-laden grass, to the chorus of all the wild birds, from skylarks high in the heavens, to the jenny wren in the hedgerows, even though the dew-laden herbage was wetting your legs more with every stride!

The younger generation of game rearers will not have experienced those days and, in a lot of ways, have missed the opportunity of being really aware of the ways of pheasant chicks. They behave very differently when being reared under a broody hen than in a brooder house, where the sheer numbers involved hide the ways and instincts of a small brood of chicks.

By and large, brooder houses are dusty places and with the heat, fine particles of feed and fluff from the birds, not the best of places to spend more time in than is essential. But on the open pheasant field there was time and pleasure in just standing and watching the antics of those lively balls of down.

It is always a good policy, should you be rearing game birds, to have all your equipment ready in good time. Should you be buying day olds or sending eggs to be hatched, don't leave the preparations until the day before the chicks are due. It is amazing how many things go wrong at the last minute if you do. Get everything set up at least a week in advance. Get the heat going and run it for a day or two. It gives you time to iron out any snags and also ensures that the unit is thoroughly warm. It is surprising how cold the nights can sometimes be in April and May and that is one thing you must avoid, young chicks getting chilled; it is a certain killer.

Don't forget the feed required. On more than one occasion I have had men rearing a hundred or two pheasants come to me to borrow a bag of food, theirs not having arrived. Order in good time. It won't cost any more, for I am sure, the good countryman that you are, you won't have many rats and mice around!

*   *   *

In April, the pheasants will start to lay, though there may be a few 'wild' birds that start late in March (a mild spell sometimes induces the birds to make an early start). Penned birds seldom lay before April, but over 50 and more years I have never known 1 April pass without finding an egg in the pens, even on one occasion in snow! Should you be producing your own eggs with penned birds it is essential that great care should be taken of the eggs. During wet weather, the eggs may be coated in mud and it is essential to remove this. In the old days, a damp cloth was used and, if the soil had dried on the shell, steel wool was the most effective thing to use. Washing in water, either tepid or cold, had been proved to effect the hatchability so was always avoided.

Today several chemicals can be used with advantage, but should you do so, it is essential to follow the instructions on the container. Nusan® is probably as good as any for this purpose and is obtainable from either a game farm or your supplier of feed. It you have a large number of eggs to deal with, an egg-washing machine is needed and the Rotomaid® is as good as any. Should you only have a few eggs, use a plastic bucket with the water at approximately the temperature shown on the washing-powder container.

The method used to hatch eggs will depend on the number involved but in any case try to ensure that the eggs are not too old before setting them. Eggs more than 1 week old lose their hatchability rapidly so endeavour to set them at least every week. Any incubator should be disinfected thoroughly before use and after each hatch. A thorough scrubbing with very hot soda water is very effective, or a spray, Thiosan®, is available. No doubt there are still some who rear only a small number of birds and still use broody hens or bantams. It is most important that the broody hens should be dusted with a disinfectant powder before the eggs are set and again after the chicks hatch. A broody will often carry lice and will be uneasy on the nest, resulting in cracked or broken eggs or, when the chicks have hatched, in trampled birds.

Even if you are only rearing a few birds, it is always advisable to order the food in plenty of time and most suppliers will be able to advise you on your requirements. There is nothing worse than chicks hatching and having no feed for them. Always get the best quality you can, this may be a bit more expensive but it usually results in fewer losses.

Having said many times how important it is to control any predators on your patch, I must emphasise that, if the weather is mild game birds often start to lay as early as March. As there is frequently little cover to hide the eggs, carrion crows and magpies will have a bonanza. Either deal with the corvids or pick up the early eggs. A pheasant has a much better chance of bringing up a brood a bit later in the season, and will always lay again if her clutch of eggs are taken before she starts to sit, but that's no reason to let the crows have them!

April is the month when you should arrange for any sowing of 'game mixture' you have in mind. There are mixtures of all sorts available for feed and cover. The right mixture will certainly attract the birds later in the year, so you must ensure that any sowing that you do is in the right place. Even a few square yards in the corner of the field will help to hold the birds. With so many hedges being uprooted these days, feed or cover can prove a big help in reducing that habit of the pheasant – straying.

If you can persuade a farmer to grow even a small patch of thousand-headed kale in a suitable spot, with a small amount of game mixture added, you should get quite a bit of sport from that patch later in the season. Unfortunately, modern methods of farming do not leave much in the way of feed or cover for game once the harvest is over. Many stubbles are ploughed up immediately. I have seen the combine

Keeping pigeons off cabbage crops, Bexley, Kent, 1936.

and the plough in one field at the same time, so any small corner that can be planted with game mixture must be an asset. A shooting farmer would probably be only too pleased to sow the odd corner but, if you rent the shoot, you may have to either pay or do the job yourself.

Much has been said, and quite a bit done, about the environment over the last few years. It is very noticeable that, on most shooting (or perhaps sporting is a better word) estates, a lot more attention is given to the environment than in many other places, but I am sure that, with the goodwill and co-operation of all people who have or rent a shoot, even where game isn't reared, much can still be done for everyone's benefit.

The people who are anti-blood sports are, in many cases, the same people who complain about the deterioration of the environment. There is no doubt that the sporting fraternity are the most likely people to make any improvements to the habitat, for the 'antis' are so often not in a position to do anything about it. During the winter, many hunts and shooting parties are pestered with the anti-blood sports people. There seems to be an increase in the number of people involved in these protests, but to me there is a great doubt if all of them really are 'anti'; in fact, I am sure many of them are not.

At one meet of the hounds, quite a gathering of protesters were present and the local police who were there became involved in dispersing them for fear of public disorder. One young lady, when questioned, said she was at University and a number of students had been provided with transport and paid £6 each to attend the meet of hounds and protest. When asked if she belonged to any 'anti' association she replied 'No, the six pounds I got for today will pay for my "cap" on Saturday. I am going hunting'. How often this 'Rent-a-Mob' happens I don't know, but I suspect quite frequently.

Although the number who are really sincere about their 'anti' views are probably comparatively small, they are able to make a lot of noise, with help, and get a lot of attention from the media. The sporting fraternity do not seem able to respond with anything positive. There must be a reason but it is not easy to find. There are many organisations which represent the many country sports, and each one does what is possible one must assume, but there appears to be nothing national that can speak with a concerted voice.

There must be millions of people interested in being able to follow their favourite sport, from fishing (and goodness knows how many are involved in that pleasant pastime), through shooting to hunting; but how many are members of any national sporting association? Quite a small percentage I would guess. Come on all you good folk who follow the country sports. Join an association that looks after your particular sport. With the vast majority of interested people belonging to an association, it should be possible to react to the antis' propaganda more effectively.

5 · MAY

W HAT A BEAUTIFUL MONTH! The countryside is looking at its best, the spring flowers giving a welcome splash of colour to the wayside and woodland after the winter. The birds are nesting and fill the air with their spring song. The summer migrants have arrived in their favoured spots, making it such a pleasure for the countryman to take an evening stroll. Unfortunately, there are not so many of these summer visitors as in bygone years. Many people have different ideas why this should be and no doubt there are many factors involved, be it fertilisers, sprays or the pulling up of hedges – in total it amounts to modern methods of farming. There is another factor, the state of the woodlands today. Gone are many of the old mixed stands of timber and with them the undergrowth of briars, privet and other low-growing shrubs. This mature timber has, in the main, been replaced by softwoods – spruce, larch and the like – often covering vast tracts of land. After the winter planting, and in the course of a year or two, all ground cover is obliterated, as the shooting fraternity know only too well. Very little wildlife is fond of the darkness and lack of insect life in this close-growing timber, another contributory factor to the decline of our once vast population of birds.

The reader may wonder what the foregoing has to do with the shooting man. Maybe as regards his sport, not all that much, but surely in the countryside a lot of pleasure stems from the wildlife to be seen, particularly the birds. Now, in my experience, a well-keepered shoot is much more likely to attract the attention of bird watchers than an area where game is not preserved. The reason, there can only be one really, is the attention paid to the control of predators. If all the folks who have a rough shoot or run an unkeepered syndicate can pay just that little bit of extra attention to dealing with crows, magpies, etc., it will be not only to their benefit but to the benefit of many, many small birds and the conservation of the countryside as well.

Now, back to the issue in most shooting men's minds – how the rearing season is going to be? In the previous chapter, I covered dealing with eggs, mainly in respect of sending them to a hatchery. If you are hatching them in your own incubator, the same procedure applies. It cannot be emphasised too much that how the eggs are treated right from the start has a great bearing on the number of chicks you are likely to hatch; in one word, the hatchability. Let's assume you are going to hatch some eggs in an incubator, large or small. The ideal (but whoever reaches the ideal?) is not to set any eggs more than 5, or at the most 7, days old. This is difficult where only a small number of stock birds are kept but maybe you know another shooting man in the same position, so why not come to an agreement with him? He may be able to let you have a number of eggs one week and you can return the compliment the next. By doing this, you will both have twice as many fresh eggs, and fresh is emphasised, every fortnight.

There are many sorts of incubators, both large and small, but they all have to be operated at the same temperature, and that is $99.5°$ Fahrenheit at the centre of the egg. The question of humidity must also be considered. Humidity is not so easy to control as the temperature and, although very important, is not quite so much so as the temperature, until the last few days of incubation. At this time, in my experience, it is almost impossible to get the humidity too high, at least in a small still-air machine. It would be fair to assume that most people who hatch and rear only a small number of pheasants, would be using a small still-air machine, with the heat supplied either by electricity or paraffin heaters. Although it is a bit more trouble, I prefer a paraffin machine as it does not provide such a dry heat and thereby helps with the humidity side of incubation. The old-fashioned Glevum® still-air machine, still around, in various sizes from 50-hen-

Putting pheasant eggs into a Glevum hatcher.

egg to 300-egg size, is probably most suitable, holding about 250 pheasant eggs, which with luck might be available from your pens and a friend's.

There are several things to consider if starting from scratch. First you need a draught-proof shed, or even garage, but don't forget the fire risk, although this is slight even if the machine is a paraffin one. Next, the machine must be level, and this is where some mistakes can be made. The part that must be level is the tray on which the eggs are set. If this is not levelled up, it will result in an uneven hatch, and an uneven hatch is seldom a good one.

The thermometer is usually suspended above the egg tray and it is important that the centre of the thermometer bulb is 2 inches from the surface of this tray; this will give the required reading at the centre of the egg. Always ensure that the wick of the paraffin heater is trimmed daily and giving a nice even steady flame, and always run the machine for several days before setting eggs, giving time for any adjustments that may be needed. When the day comes to set the eggs, it may be useful to remember that pheasant eggs take 24 days to hatch, so if you want to be available when hatching day comes, you can set the eggs according to your commitments. The eggs should be marked with a circle on one side of the egg joined by a line to a cross on the other. When the eggs have been incubation for 24 hours, the tray should be taken from the machine and the eggs 'moved' along the line, i.e. if the circle is uppermost when setting, turn the egg until the cross is at the top. This operation should be done twice a day at approximately 12-hour intervals, at which point the eggs are moved back to their original positions. At about the fifth day, a small dish of hot water should be placed on the chick compartment of the incubator to boost humidity and this should be kept filled until the chicks hatch.

On the twenty-first day, the eggs should no longer be turned, but humidity should be built up by placing wet cloths or cotton wool in front of the eggs or even by spraying the eggs with a very fine spray of hot water. Once the eggs chip, do not open the incubator until the bulk appears to have hatched; then is the time to let the chicks down into the drying-off tray, after removing the dish of water, where they can remain for 12 hours or more. With luck and good management, you could have an 85 or even 90 per cent hatch. If you don't, don't blame me blame the machine!

These days, it is fairly easy to rear pheasant chicks, particularly in small numbers, using one of the many heating systems and ensuring the chicks are in a draught-proof shed or building. With the best feed being used, no problems should arise. At the first sign of feather pecking, the readily-available plastic bits must be used and, in 6 weeks, you should have good strong healthy poults. Next month will be soon enough to talk about what to do next.

A few words about ducks. A lot of people, in particular wildfowlers, like to rear a few mallard. It is not advisable to try to hatch ducks in a small still-air incubator; even gamekeepers tend to fight shy of this. If you do want the fun and have the facilities to rear your own ducks, it would be advisable to buy them as day olds. After the first week, ducks are less trouble to rear than pheasants, needing little heat except at night, and thriving on a much cheaper diet. One thing that must be avoided – water! No, they must have water to drink of course, but do not let them have access to water more than $\frac{1}{2}$ inch deep unless the container is filled with stones, Ducks will easily drown until they have their feathers, which provide the oil and buoyancy. Normally this comes from the brooding duck.

* * *

Very soon many thousands of pheasant chicks will be hatched, both by incubator and hen pheasant. Now we need a good spell of suitable weather to enable the 'little balls of fluff' to thrive and grow into strong healthy poults. The weather does not have quite the same importance when chicks are being reared under artificial heat but oh! what an important factor it is for those hatched by the mother bird!

Unfortunately, Man cannot do anything about the weather – or is it really a good thing that we can't? Sometimes the month of May is ideal for game chicks, not too hot, not too cold and not too wet, but much more often the weather is far from ideal when the chicks are hatching.

Many syndicates and rough shoots rely to a very large degree on

Newly hatched pheasant chicks after their shells have been removed.

wild-hatched birds. A really bad spell of weather when they are hatching can make the following shooting season almost a disaster. For this very reason, there are many more people rearing a small number of pheasants and, in some cases, partridges as well. There is no need to go into detail about rearing, this has been dealt with before, not only in earlier chapters but in numerous other publications. It is, of course, a good thing to rear game to release on a shoot, even if the people do not get the return they hoped for. The predators will take their share (very often too high a share!); some will die, the poachers will have some and a number will stray some considerable distance from the release point. The birds that stray will probably provide sport for someone, and maybe encourage them to rear a few themselves, and don't forget you will probably have some birds straying onto your shoot!

I was pleased to see a letter from Mr Michael Swan of the Game Conservancy at Fordingbridge, referring to the figure of 37 per cent returns that I once gave for round about the 1950s. It is most encouraging to know that it is now around 41 per cent, due, to a large degree, to the research and advice of the staff at Fordingbridge. They should be supported by all shooting men.

Yes, the more people who rear pheasants, the better it is for all those who enjoy the sport. Even a small number reared and released by a farmer can make an almost blank day into an enjoyable one. If you can persuade a farmer to do this on your shoot, be it an unkeepered one, it can make quite a difference. Almost certainly that farmer will take a greater interest in the game on his 'patch'. Ask him to shoot on one of your days. He will enjoy it and you will have another pair of eyes keeping watch when you are not there.

Eggs may be a bit scarce to the man in a small way but, late in the season, towards the end of May, many large keepered shoots have 'set' all the eggs they need but still have some hens in the laying pens. By asking the man in charge, it is possible to get these late eggs for a song or maybe for nothing. Don't expect the same hatchability from them but if they have cost little you should be amply rewarded for your work with the incubator.

My late employer once said to me 'Don't waste any eggs. If we have more than we need, encourage the small man by giving him a sitting or two'. What a help this was to a number of people over the years. Hopefully other large estates carry out this practice. It can only do good. For many years now, the shooting of game has not been the preserve of the wealthy landed gentry. In fact, there is probably a larger head of game shot on the syndicates and small shoots, could they be added up, than that killed on the large private estates. Even some of the large estates are let as a whole, or in part, to syndicate shooters.

In the last chapter, I mentioned seeing what was almost certainly a chiff-chaff in January, and remarked about the unusual things that can be seen in the countryside by an alert and observant watcher. Many years ago, whilst watching the young pheasants make their leisurely way back to their home covert one fine September evening, I saw a hare gradually grazing its way along the meadow. Obviously hares must cover a lot of ground whilst feeding, often having a few bites at some favourite grass or herbage and then moving on to the next tasty morsel. This hare was doing just that. Suddenly, and without any indication from other birds, or even the young pheasants, a hen sparrow hawk appeared and swooped at the hare. The fur flew and the hare, although it did not squeal, made off at some speed. The hawk, however, made another pass at the now fast-moving 'puss'. Once again it dislodged a large cloud of fur, this time causing the luckless hare to squeal in alarm, put on speed and disappear into the wood. I had not seen such an incident before or, for that matter, since.

Whilst talking about hares, another incident comes to mind. Leaning over a gate one day (keepers have the reputation of doing a lot of leaning over gates), a hare appeared over the brow of a hill, put up by a cowman rounding up his herd to be milked. I had earlier seen a weasel in and out of a hedge bottom, busily hunting for mice, but this creature had disappeared from view as the hare came steadily towards the gate where I was standing. Sensing an unusual object in the gateway, the hare, not travelling at all fast, turned and made for a small gap in hedge. The next second there was an ear-piercing squeal from the hare. My first thoughts were that it had hit a snare which had been set unbeknown to me. However that was not the case, for the hare was soon jumping and pouncing about in the field. In a very short while, it ceased to squeal and lay kicking on the grass. On approaching the now almost-lifeless animal, a small object could be seen holding on tight to the hare, just behind one ear. It was a weasel! No doubt the one seen earlier, which must have been up in the hedge and pounced on the unsuspecting hare as it went through the gap. Once again, never before had I seen this and never since.

* * *

Recently, whilst talking to a friend on the phone, the question of 'mutant' pheasants was raised – 'mutes' as we used to call them. A man who had some rough shooting had been rearing a few pheasants to increase his sport and had, for a number of years, kept a small stock of hen birds from the rearing. Being in a small way, and with his wife doing most of the feeding, they both became attached to the birds and often kept one or two for a second and even a third season. This practice is not always advisable for a number of reasons. The eggs laid are usually very hatchable, though there are not so many of them. Perhaps I should give other reasons for not keeping stock birds for a second year and the cost of feed must be the main reason. There is also the risk of disease, which must be much greater when birds are kept in a confined area for a long while, which no doubt was the case of the chap who brought up the question of 'mutants'. He was amazed to notice that one of his hen birds had taken on a lot of a cock bird's characteristics, namely an almost black head, numerous brown patches and a very definite barred tail. This is something that is not really rare but, nevertheless, rather unusual and a hen bird will sometimes change so much that, unless closely inspected, it will look just like a cock bird. A cock pheasant changing to a hen is in my experience much rarer and, in either case, the one thing that is common to each is the tail. In what must be a sex change, the hen-turned-cock and the cock-turned-hen always retain the same size tail with just the difference in basic colouring.

When rearing a lot of pheasants, there will nearly always be one or two first-year mutants per 1,000 reared, which isn't of any con-sequence. Should the number increase to seven, eight or nine per 1,000, it may be advisable to seek a change of blood. Today, with so many people rearing a few pheasants, it should be no trouble to get eggs to change the blood. It is doubtful if it is really necessary where large numbers are reared. In years gone by, large estates always changed a large number of cock birds, but maybe it was only an excuse for the keepers to have a day out on a distant estate!

No doubt many readers will have noticed how tame pheasants become on 2 February! It isn't a myth by any means. I have noted it over the last 50 years! Pheasants, particularly cock birds, will show up in places where they have not been found before, strutting about with much less fear of a human being than during the shooting season and often with a number of hen birds for company. Now it is obvious that birds don't know what day of the month it is, although they will know the breeding season is nigh and will be preparing for that. There seems to be no logical reason why so many birds should show up in various places immediately the shooting season is over. I don't think it is something the shooting man imagines, for only this year, several people, not even interested in country sports, have mentioned it to me.

May is such a wonderful month in the country. With all the young fresh greenery and many wild flowers in bloom, it is inevitable that many town dwellers will be out and about. Ninety per cent of these people do no harm at all, so long as they keep to the footpaths and, should they have a dog with them, keep it on a lead. Nevertheless that 10 per cent of thoughtless people, because it is nearly always that, can do a large amount of damage to the game population.

In May, many game birds will be sitting and, in almost every case, should that bird be put off the nest by a dog, the eggs will be deserted. Sometimes, but not always, more eggs will be laid, but rarely as many and, even then it would be a late hatch.

On more than one occasion I have asked people to keep their dog on a lead whilst walking a footpath. Most have done so, but only after a long explanation for the reason. With being used to letting 'Fido' have a run in a town park, they find it difficult to see what damage their pet can do in the wide open spaces of the countryside. I have found that a polite approach, with a full explanation usually makes these visitors to the rural areas follow the Country Code.

Stray dogs in the countryside have been more numerous, and dogs straying with their masters as well, since so many townspeople have moved out into the villages to live, so it falls to the farmers, people with sporting rights and gamekeepers to educate these people on what is so essential for the good of all wildlife and not only any game in the area.

By now, a lot of game chicks will be in the early stages of rearing. The first 10 days are probably the most important. Feed these days is no problem, plenty of high protein 'crumbs' being available, but heat is probably the greatest reason for any losses and it can be either too little or too much heat. Too little heat will cause the 'balls of fluff' to crowd on top of one another, with some getting smothered and others chilled. Too much heat will make the chicks push to the extremes of their confined space, again, often ending in some getting smothered. There is also the risk of complete failure of the heating system and a wise man is prepared for this. Where only a small number of chicks are involved, boxing them in chick boxes and taking them even to a warm room in the house will minimise the risk of chilling, but don't overload the chick boxes or they will smother.

Many large shoots have alternative heating, such as a generator, or

Pheasant chicks in a brooder.

should I say a source of power, ready for any failure in the electricity supply. This is too costly for anyone rearing only a few hundreds. A paraffin heater can be most useful in a small rearing unit, but make sure it has a good supply of fuel and that the wick is ready trimmed. It is advisable to have this ready before the chicks are put into the unit because one never knows. Much valuable time can be lost trimming the wick and filling the heater with fuel. It is not a bad idea to keep the heater in the unit, if room is available. This can mean that you only have to maintain the heat in the hut and not start almost from scratch and build it up. Always be aware of the risk of fire; don't turn the wick too high in your haste to keep those precious little 'sporting shots' of the future warm!

When rearing pheasants under modern conditions and methods, some people overlook the fact that the birds need grit. It is probable that not as much is required with the modern feeds. Crumbs and pellets do not need the same digesting as hard seeds or grain. Nevertheless, it is essential that a supply of grit is readily available. Make sure that it is of the size suitable to the chicks. Various sizes are obtainable but 'chick grit', a fairly fine-cut flint, is all right until the birds are 6 or 8 weeks old. Usually at this age, they will be moved to the coverts and a larger grit is then used. Birds will only take the size of grit and, I sometimes think, the shape, which they like. Even if there still seems some available to them, make sure more is added each week at least.

One never knows what sort of season it will be for rearing game birds but, with modern techniques and food, there is no reason why it shouldn't be successful.

*   *   *

In May, hundreds of thousands of game bird chicks will be hatched, but how many will reach maturity? The figure is impossible to arrive at, of course. The wild partridge usually rears a large percentage of its chicks, given a reasonably good environment and a minimum of predators. The pheasant in the wild state is naturally a poor mother, which rears only a very small number of its brood. No matter what the environment, few wild hen pheasants rear more than two or three of the chicks hatched. A good spring and summer, weatherwise, is essential for a good 'crop' of wild game birds, which is basically what many small rough shoots rely on.

With so many factors stacked against any quantity of game being reared in the wild, it is not surprising that more and more 'small' batches of birds are being reared up and down the country. It is so much easier to rear game today than in the past. Most interested persons can do so.

When I started as a lad with the gamekeepers over 50 years ago, the rearing of pheasants, partridges and ducks was a major and expensive operation. Thus, only wealthy landowners were able to enjoy game shooting on any scale. Broody hens were used for rearing. The chicks were reared on large open bird fields; sometimes, there would be 400 or 500 coops, each with broody hen and chicks, on one large field. It had to be a large field for it needed 1 acre for every 10 coops. I can't see any farmer allowing his land to be put to that use for at least 2 months in the summer in these days.

The percentage reared to 6 weeks old was much lower than is expected from the modern brooder house, or even small rearing unit. At twenty chicks per broody, it was considered an excellent result if fifteen poults were taken to the wood at 6 weeks old. Seventy five per cent was then good, but today would be classed as verging on a poor result. There were many factors in those days that do not apply now. Right from the start, disease was a distinct possibility. Broody hens would be gathered from over a wide area and many had been living in far from ideal conditions. A number would die whilst brooding the eggs, mostly from unknown diseases. Disease often showed up on the pheasant chicks later on. As much care as possible was taken to eliminate trouble of this sort but really there wasn't enough known about such things in those days.

The broodies were dusted with a disinfectant powder, Keatings Lice Powder® I think it was called, but this only dealt with the lice and there was little that could be done to combat disease, except cleanliness. The 'sitting boxes' were either lime washed or creosoted each year before use, as were the coops. The lime wash was made by slaking lump lime with cold water, which caused it to boil. It was reckoned lime so treated helped to sterilise the boxes and coops when brushed on. Dealing with a large amount of equipment meant a lot of hard work which, in view of later knowledge, may well have been in vain.

When disease did strike on the bird field, any method adopted usually depended on the whim or fancy of the keeper in charge. In fact very little was at all effective. Gapes was probably the most obvious disease. Some men swore by spirit of camphor in the drinking water. Others dusted the chicks with a mixture of carbolic acid and powdered lime! The carbolic was mixed with the lime and, when the lime was dry and powdery again, it was blown into the closed coop with bellows, making the occupants sneeze. This sneezing was supposed to make the young birds eject the gape worms from the windpipe! Special bellows could be purchased for this purpose, but there is much doubt whether all the labour involved was worth it. If the chicks did not appear to be thriving as they should, some keepers would mix a 'tonic' with the feed, and often the ingredients of such a tonic were 'secret'. Maybe some did some good but they cannot compare with the modern drugs that are available for almost every ailment a game bird may suffer from.

Those days of long ago meant many hours spent looking after the game chicks. Not only were there problems of disease but an alert watch had to be kept for the ever-present predators. Despite all this, they were happy days and there was much to be observed, the like of which is never seen in a modern brooder house!

With modern rearing methods on a large or a small scale, it is probably more important than ever to maintain a high degree of hygiene. You may have 100 or 200 young birds in a comparatively small area and any infection could clear the lot in no time at all. Fortunately, there are many things available today which can eliminate most of the risks; some are expensive, yes, but you wouldn't say that if you lost several hundred month-old poults! Last month, I said take great care of the eggs. Now May is with us, take great care of the chicks, and there is no better place to start than making sure that all the equipment you will use has been thoroughly disinfected. There is no need for me to go into this too much, for if you get your disinfectant from a reputable provider of game-rearing equipment, you will be able to get instructions on how and when to use it.

I remember an incident, a number of years ago, when my employer's wife asked me to hatch some pea-hen eggs and rear the resulting chicks with a broody hen. I was reluctant to do so, as there would soon be several thousand pheasant chicks in the brooder houses. However when the 'boss' said he would be responsible for any mishap, I agreed. The eggs duly hatched and the chicks were put in a small independent run as far as possible from the brooder houses. A week or so later, the batch of chicks nearest to the broody hen's run were showing signs of distress and action had to be taken. It was pretty obvious that an outbreak of coccidiosis had occurred but fortunately, by prompt action, only a small number of chicks were lost and the disease was contained. There was no proof of course, but that broody hen was blamed for the problem! One cannot be too careful when rearing chicks of any breed.

Broodies seem quite a large part of this so I'll carry on with that

Some keepers still like to use broodies.

theme. In the mid 1930s, when motor transport became more readily available, we used to be able to travel further afield looking for the large number of sitting hens we needed. On one occasion, we had ranged some distance from base, calling on any likely-looking farms as we went. A nice tidy farm appeared as we travelled the country and a large hen house was to be seen. As we pulled into the yard, the farmer appeared and inquired what we wanted. On telling him we were after broody hens, he said 'Come on, I've got plenty'. (At 4s. each no doubt he was tempted.) As we got to the poultry houses, he said 'Give us your bag'. Rather reluctantly, we gave him a couple of sacks; normally we liked to take the hens off their nests ourselves. He came out of the hen house with full sacks and we duly counted the hens and paid him. Later that evening (we always went after broodies in the evening), we were putting our haul onto the already-prepared nests and artificial eggs, when my mate George shouted to me 'Hey 'owd un, we've got some good sitters tonight'. 'Well that's what we've been after', I replied. 'Come and have a look at these', he said. I walked down to where he was and, as I did so, he lifted up a couple of lids of the nest boxes. 'What do you reckon of them', he says, pointing to the two occupants. The large Rhode Island Reds seemed to be sitting tight, so I bent down and lifted them off the nest. They were nothing but feathers and bone! 'I told you we had some good sitters', says George. 'They are too weak to stand up'. These particular birds had come from the farm where the old lad had insisted on bagging them himself, so you can guess we didn't go there again!

6 · JUNE

HOW HAVE THE PHEASANT EGGS HATCHED? If you have been trying your hand with an incubator, you have had good results it is hoped, but it is not too late to put in another batch of eggs if they are still available. These later batches rarely hatch as well as the early eggs but, as long as you don't expect quite the same results, they are often the best bet for many small shoots. As long as the chicks are well fed, on the best-quality crumbs and mini-pellets, they are often the cheapest way of stocking the shoot. Being later, the length of time they have to be fed is shorter, thus reducing the feed bill quite a lot. As a rough guide, 100 full-grown pheasants need about 1 hundredweight of grain a week. If you have 200 or 300 full-grown birds needing feeding for a month or more before you intend to shoot, $\frac{1}{2}$ ton of feed has to be found. At today's prices, that is quite an item on a small working man's shoot. Eggs hatched in late June will produce full-grown pheasants by, at the latest, the end of October and really that is early enough to start covert shooting. Good luck if you decide to hatch a later one or two; they will probably help out later in the season in any case.

Having discussed late-hatched pheasants, what happened to the stock birds out of the laying pens? Many a pheasant has been taken from the laying pen and turned out into what has been thought to be a good wood on the shoot. This is almost always a complete waste. These released stock birds seldom stay in that wood. If they have been

Pheasant with a leather strap brail.

'brailed' in the laying pen, few of them will go to roost. They are thus pretty certain to become the prey of that wide-ranging animal, Reynard. You may be certain that there are no foxes on your shoot, but at this time of the year, with well-grown cubs, the fox will travel great distances, with the ever-increasing need for food for the growing litter. In any case, foxes usually hunt some distance from the cubs. Many litters of cubs have been reared in a rabbit warren, with the rabbits literally undisturbed. If you have a number of stock birds to release, it is better, if at all possible, to treat them exactly as if you were releasing poults. If, after several days in a pen, just a few are given their freedom, they nearly always try and get back into the pen. By letting them out slowly, there is a much better chance of them remaining in the wood.

A lot has been said about ex-pen pheasants rearing a chick or two after they have been released, but this depends on so many factors. Released properly and early (you might forgo that last batch in the incubator) and under really ideal conditions, a few chicks may be hatched, but don't forget mother has got to rear them even then! With plenty of ideal cover, plenty of natural feed and a good spell of weather at the right time, there might possibly be a few more targets come the shooting season. The shoots where sprays are seldom used are more likely to produce this late crop of pheasants as there will be more feed, insects, seeds and the like.

It may well be better to try and ensure that at least the birds from the laying pens survive to the shooting season, so treat them like poults. Some people are in the habit of buying pheasants ex-laying pens and most game farms advertise them. You may even consider selling your birds when you have as many eggs as you want. The money no doubt would come in useful for that ever increasing essential feed!

Whilst writing about laying pen pheasants and poults, I remembered, and it may seem an unusual connection, the first pheasant I shot. Many years ago, when large numbers of game birds were reared on many estates, it was not unusual to see fields and fields full of coops. As may be guessed, these large fields, with literally thousands of young pheasants running about, were very prone to frequent visits from a varied assortment of predators. These could range from rat, stoat, weasel, cat and fox on the ground to hawk, crow, magpie, jay and seagulls from the air. Those old keepers had to be pretty vigilant men if they were to be successful. Usually they knew, almost by a casual glance, what had been raiding the coops. The story being related was a bit different. It had been noticed that one particular coop had lost a number of its chicks. The broody hen was a good mother, so she was not to blame. Some hens, after hatching successfully and sometimes brooding the chicks for several days, would, without any obvious reason, turn cannibal and devour all their families. This particular broody was a 'good un' and there was no apparent reason for the chicks to disappear. Being only a lad at the time, I was detailed to take up a position by this particular coop to try and ascertain the reason for the chicks disappearing. The lads always got these what appeared to be thankless jobs but, on looking back, it was probably a very good way to learn the ways of predators, and there was plenty of time to observe other items of natural history, insects and plants.

After watching the coop for what seemed hours and hours, without the slightest indication of a predator about, no piping from a blackbird to warn of ground vermin, no *tink, tink, tink* from a chaffinch to give notice of attack from the air, a larger movement of the waving grass than normal was seen. Watching very closely, and half expecting a cat or a young cub to appear, nothing could be seen. The brooding hen gave no warning cry to the chicks, even though the movement was right in front of the coop. What could it be? Was it advisable to walk and see what it was? No, it might disappear into the long grass. Whilst he was thus pondering, what should appear alongside the coop but a hen pheasant! Relax, that's not the culprit. Relaxing was almost a mistake for, at that very moment, a pheasant chick ran round the coop right into the hen pheasant who immediately pecked at it, killed it and started to throw it up into the air in an attempt to pull it to pieces. There could now be no doubt that this was the reason for the number of chicks in this particular coop failing. There was only one thing to be done; shoot it. So, as soon as the pheasant moved off into the grass, it was up with the gun and, taking careful aim to be absolutely sure, 'bang'. Another problem solved. No more chicks went missing from that coop, so without a shadow of doubt that hen pheasant was the culprit. Pheasants are at times cannibals, as has become evident with the modern intensive rearing. Keep your eye on the chicks!

*   *   *

In pre-war days practically all pheasants were reared on large estates and large fields full of coops were quite a common sight. It was hard, trying work in those days. The coops were spaced 20 yards apart each way and the chicks had to be fed four times a day. That meant a lot of tramping through long wet grass. There was no real waterproof clothing so, most days, the keeper could be sure of getting wet. Try walking through long grass at dusk after a blazing hot day; the rising dew seems more penetrating than any rain!

Today, rearing game birds is so much more comfortable. There are no problems about the food but it was rather hit or miss in the old days. Each keeper had his own ideas about what was best for his chicks but no idea about protein content of the food.

Nearly all keepers started the chicks off with hard-boiled egg and

Young pheasants, five weeks old, in rearing pen. The food trough, bottom right, has a cover to keep the food dry.

some sort of meal. No doubt this was high in protein but after the first 4 or 5 days, these chicks received a really mixed diet, from fine-cut maize to boiled hemp seed.

Some pheasant-rearing fields were always classed better than others, though seldom was the same field used 2 years running. Looking back, one field was probably better than another because of its herbage, not because of the herbage itself, but the insect life it supported. There is no doubt that insects are a source of high protein and many birds rely entirely on a good supply, particularly during the early days of a fledgling's life.

Today, it is possible to get a compound feed for game birds which contains all the essentials for healthy growth, right down to the trace elements. The feed is obtainable in so many forms that, at all stages in a game-bird's growth, it is possible to feed the correct balanced diet: starting with 'crumbs', going on to 'mini pellets', and then through various other pellets, until the chick becomes a poult, when a change can be made to grain, preferably a good quality wheat.

83

This is a vast difference to the old days when so much of the food had to be boiled. Many keepers continued to boil the feed right up to the first shoot. Wheat and cut maize was the most popular feed, boiled in an army-type boiler until soft. What a job that was! It needed continual stirring to prevent the maize in particular from sticking to the side of the boiler, where it would soon burn! Not much fun on a wet day when the fire was reluctant to burn; it then took ages before the brew was cooked. The old keepers maintained that feeding their charges this boiled feed helped to keep them at home. There may be something in this; boiled corn contains a large amount of water, probably 50 per cent. A crop full of this would obviously be digested quicker than a crop full of dry hard grain. Thus the bird would be ready for a feed much sooner. Some say a hungry bird strays, but the majority make their way to where they know a feed is, or soon will be, available – namely the feed track!

Don't think that I consider this old method of feeding superior to today's methods – I don't. Many shoots could not exist under those old conditions and, by and large, modern feeds and modern methods provide good high-flying pheasants in the right place at the right time. There aren't many records of percentages killed in the old days, only the total bags. One reason was the old keepers never told anyone, least of all their bosses, how many pheasants had been reared, so the keeper might have an idea how things had gone but no one else!

It is probably true that a larger percentage is being returned than was the case years ago, so modern methods are certainly successful and, if only an improvement in habitat can be maintained, shooting will continue to thrive.

I don't know why I have gone on about the old days compared with the 1980s but a month ago I was visiting a large shoot and the keepers were fine and busy getting the brooder houses ready. Many tools were in evidence, hammers, pliers, screwdrivers and even a power saw! This brought home to me the vast changes that have taken place in these last 20 years. The keepers' skills seem of necessity to be much different today. It doesn't seem quite so important to be a naturalist, a good trapper and observer. Today other skills are needed: joiner, electrician, plumber and, by the look of some of the incubators, it won't be long before a keeper will have to be a computer expert as well!

A very good old friend of mine, and a great country lover, Alec Minshull, is very concerned about the large number of animals and birds killed by the modern traffic on our roads. A heavy toll of wildlife is lost in this way, but I suppose one has to be sensible about this. It is obviously unwise to take evasive action if, say, a badger crossed the road in the glare of your headlights, or you might find yourself through a hedge! We agreed eventually that much of this carnage of modern times was unavoidable, but he then produced a photograph of an owlet, almost certainly a tawny owl, perched on a lad's wrist. Alec knew nothing of the background of the photograph, but guessed that the bird was being reared as a pet. 'Now what does the Crow (the author's nickname) think of that?' he asked.

Even today, lads will take these young birds from the nest and try to rear them. Many fail and the bird dies, very often because of lack of knowledge of the fledgling's needs. Many more are picked up under nests from which they have fallen (jackdaws and rooks are particularly prone to this) and, of course, many owls nest in lofts and old buildings, making it easy to obtain a young bird.

Fledglings picked up after falling from the nest may seem pathetic things and in need of help, but folks would do much better to leave them entirely alone. Often the parent bird will continue to feed them until such time as they can look after themselves. If they don't attend to their young, the youngster will certainly die – a natural cull. If a person takes it home and does rear it successfully, what is to become of it? It is no life for a wild bird in a cage and, if released, it will almost certainly die, not knowing how to obtain food for itself after a long period of regular feeds in captivity. Owls in particular have little chance of survival.

I know someone will say 'The bird I reared still comes to the garden'. Maybe, but this is the exception rather than the rule. The time is almost on us when these young birds will be about. Please, never take one from its nest; never pick one up from under its nest, despite your feelings for the poor little thing. Some will live, some will die, but the casualties are part of nature's way of balancing itself.

*   *   *

By now there will be many thousands, nay probably millions of pheasant chicks in brooder houses up and down the country, with many young partridges and ducks also. A good many folk responsible for the rearing of these 'shots of the future', will be scratching their heads and wondering why the chicks aren't doing as well as they should. There can be many reasons for them not thriving as they should.

Much has been written over the years about the essentials required to rear game birds and it is not really necessary to repeat these comments. There must, however, be a large amount of equipment in use that is not meeting the demanding standards required to have a really successful rearing season. The makeshift rearing unit is often less successful than one produced by a reputable firm, but the cost of such a unit, be it only a small one, may be beyond the purse of the man in a small way. So long as attention is paid to detail it is quite possible to be happy with the results should, say, only 85 per cent of the chicks hatched be taken to wood at 6 weeks.

A crate of young pheasants being taken to the release pen in the wood.

The head scratching mentioned when the chicks aren't thriving, may be due to reasons other than makeshift equipment. With a high density of livestock, especially young livestock, there is always a high risk of disease. If conditions are not quite right, the risk is higher. There are so many things that young pheasants and partridge are prone to. *Anyone* in the business of game rearing should get a booklet on the subject, which no doubt the Game Conservancy at Fordingbridge would be only too happy to supply.

Many of the diseases are quite difficult to detect, at least in the early stages. One or two, such as coccidiosis, can go through a batch like wildfire, unless spotted early and the proper antidote given. Gapes is probably the easiest disease to spot and should be no problem once the readily available drug is given.

Quite recently, there was an outbreak of fowl pest (Newcastle disease). An appeal went out for all gamekeepers to stop the movement of stock birds, so it could be quite possible for this disease to appear again during this rearing season. It would really be advisable, should you have the slightest doubt about the welfare of your game birds, to call in a veterinary surgeon, preferably one who specialises in bird diseases. It could save a lot of birds for you as well as your neighbours.

The following may not be of particular interest to the shooting man but, although it is basically a farming problem, it should be of interest to the sportsman in general. It is about lambs and a problem that, as far as I am aware, remains unsolved. During the lambing season on a farm in North Wales, in the 'teens of lambs were found dead over a period of a week or so. Now these lambs were about a week old when they were turned out with the ewes onto a meadow close to a stream. The ewes had been lambed under cover and so their offspring were quite strong and frisky when released into the meadow.

It appears that, during the night, something had been amongst the flock and killed a lamb. A week-old lamb is quite big and usually pretty active but, on each occasion, when a dead lamb was found, it had not been eaten or even bitten into. The cause or apparent cause of death in every case was a crushed skull. The whole skull was crushed, as if battered with a heavy object, and the only sign of blood was a small hole at the side of the neck.

The farmer was and still is completely baffled by the way these lambs have been killed. Shepherding for many years, he obviously has seen a lot of lambs killed by all sorts of methods and animals, but never like this. There are foxes in the area, but he has lost few lambs to them, always lambing the flock in the buildings. Normally a fox will take a lamb as it is being born, if this happens at night in the fields, and in any case, a fox usually has a meal of his kill. No, he is certain a fox was not to blame for the deaths and just as certain that a badger was not responsible, there being no signs of badger tracks, not only around the dead lambs, but around the farm.

The small hole, from which it appears the blood has been sucked, makes one think of the weasel family, but to me it seems doubtful if even a large polecat or mink would be capable of crushing a lamb's skull to the extent that seems to happen. I suppose it is possible that more than one animal is involved in the slaughter, maybe two of one doing the killing, perhaps for the sake of it, and another beastie coming along and sucking the blood.

The farmer kept watch on his flock after several losses, but despite spending a large part of the night on patrol, the losses continued, though not on quite such a large scale. I have not seen any of these lambs after they have been killed, the farm being quite some distance from my residence, but the facts are, without doubt, as stated. An inspection of a corpse may be helpful, but apparently the farmer's vet is at a complete loss to even suggest what has killed the lamb. Any ideas anyone? I should be only too pleased to pass any information on to the farmer concerned, who might then be able to take some precautions for another lambing season.

More years ago than I care to remember, I was faced with a somewhat similar problem. It was in late July, with a large number of pheasant poults in this particular wood, and they had just started to go to roost. One morning I found a partially-eaten bird and was very doubtful which predator had killed it. It did not appear to be a tawny owl, for they will kill pheasant poults at the roosting stage, and it certainly wasn't a fox or for that matter a fox cub. I have seen far too many killed by that animal over the years. The next morning another poult lay dead, this time beneath a bush in which a number roosted.

Still I was perplexed about the 'varmit' responsible. This went on for almost a fortnight, sometimes one and sometimes a couple every morning, but not a real clue that would account for what was responsible. The culprit never returned to the kill, always preferring warm flesh the next night.

The method used to kill the bird did seem a bit like a stoat's work, but only vaguely so. However eventually the mystery was solved, when one morning what should be in one of the tunnel traps but a polecat. This was the first polecat ever taken or known to be on this particular estate, so none of the keepers had experienced the ways of this animal.

Since then there has been a large increase in this animal and they seem to be fairly common over a large area. Being mainly nocturnal, they are seldom seen, unless they are hard pushed when rearing a family, when daylight forays will be made. I hope you don't get a litter of polecats near your birds when you take them to cover!

*　　*　　*

A few weeks ago I was the speaker at the annual dinner of a local agricultural discussion group and a most enjoyable evening it was. Many of the farmers were naturally interested in field sports, in fact some of them farmed the land over which the Blue Riband of coursing, the Waterloo Cup, is run. One of the guests was a local gamekeeper, Ian Grindy, who asked a few questions about old-time keeping.

Eventually I was asked for my views on modern-day keepers. I had to say that they had it easy compared with pre-war men. Ian didn't take too kindly to this, considering that keepers of today are under greater pressure from many directions, which is true up to a point.

Let's go briefly into the life of a keeper 50 years ago. He would almost certainly live in an isolated cottage, more than likely without piped water, with oil lamps for lights and no sewerage. Most of today's keepers have modern houses with all conveniences and often close to the village, if not in it. No carrying of water, filling and trimming lamps, or emptying the outside 'loo' for them. That's the difference in living conditions, but what about the working conditions? Rarely did an old velveteen have any transport; if he was lucky he had a pony and trap, but most had to manage with a cycle. Today (and I agree it is essential) he can ride around his patch in a Land Rover or other four-wheeled vehicle. This makes it easier to transport feed and equipment to wherever needed. I can remember having to carry $\frac{1}{2}$ hundredweight of wheat nearly $\frac{1}{2}$ mile every morning to feed an outlying covert. Today, the keeper would go in the vehicle and, incidentally, probably miss any signs of nocturnal activities!

When it comes to rearing game with modern incubators and brooder houses, there can be no comparison with the old method of broody hens and the open bird field. Ian says 'There is a lot at stake if an incubator fails with several thousand eggs in it', but it is possible to retrieve that situation. I remember at least two occasions when the rearing field was flooded by an unusually heavy thunderstorm, and even several coops were floating in the storm water! No way of retrieving that and it was almost impossible to buy in poults as

Broody hens hatching pheasant eggs on the Game Farm. This is not often seen now.

replacements. Yes, Ian, the estate owners were probably more understanding when such acts of God took place, but they still expected a good show come the shooting season.

During the shooting season, the modern keeper has a much better chance of going to other shoots, something pre-war keepers could rarely do, transport being the main problem. A shoot 20 or even 50 miles away is within range today, but it wasn't for the old lad on his bike with the dog running beside him, so he was restricted to shoots very close by. Going to 'pick up' often gives the modern keeper ideas which may prove useful, provides useful contacts with other keepers and must be an advantage. It was usually the head keeper who went to other shoots in pre-war days and then it was mostly to act as loader to his employers.

Predators seemed to be a much greater problem in those days than they are now, particularly on the pheasant field. It required a permanent watch to be kept, for even a weasel could very quickly wipe out a coop of twenty young birds. Has anyone ever tried to spot a weasel in a hay field! There was always some animal or bird raiding the young pheasants as easy feed for their clamouring young. They were almost like wasps round a honey pot. All this despite the fact that a year-round battle went on 'twixt keeper and predator. I have only heard of one incident where a stoat killed a number of pheasant poults in a brooder-house run, but that was soon dealt with. A modern keeper can leave a brooder house for long periods, so long as heat, food and water are available for the inmates; no feeding by hand four times a day. I can assure you, Ian, it was a relief to move the poults to the wood after 6 weeks of long wet grass, and there was no real waterproof clothing either.

Many tasks befell the pre-war keeper that are not done today. Take the rabbit population. Today, there are comparatively small numbers about in some places but, in the 1930s, there were literally thousands and, on most estates, it was the keeper's duty to reduce these to reasonable numbers. This meant much hard work. Netting, ferreting, snaring and trapping may be sport to some people but, when you are doing it week in and week out on top of many other duties, it is no longer a pleasure.

Trapping was probably the heaviest work, for each keeper would probably be using around four dozen of the old gin trap, now banned. They would be set in burrows, looked at twice a day and moved every 5 days. Forty-eight traps were as much as anyone wanted to carry and it would take a full day to set them. Many rabbit holes had to be firmly stopped, which in some situations could be really hard work. The next morning there could be anything up to thirty rabbits to carry, often quite a distance, to the game larder.

Snaring was easier work, but many keepers made their own snares and had to cut the pegs. A hundred was the usual 'set' and these had to be checked, after dark and early morning. Ferreting was resorted to in the less accessible places where traps could not be set, but was no pleasure to the old-time keeper for it could be time consuming and less productive than other methods. Long netting at night was often a dual-purpose operation. If it was a good night to net rabbits it was a good night to catch poachers, so rather than sit about in the cold waiting for the poachers to appear, many keepers preferred to net rabbits themselves and often catch the rabbit poachers at the same time.

I remember once running a long net out down the side of a wood and met a poacher doing the same thing coming from the other direction. The amusing thing was he thought I was poaching too and offered to share the catch with me!

Another keeper and myself once took a bet, for a bottle of whisky (12s. 6d. in those days), that we couldn't catch 1,000 rabbits in a week, from Saturday night to Saturday night. We set about the job with relish and, by snaring, setting 200 snares, long netting at night and using a line ferret in small burrows after driving the wood, managed to reach our target in 6 days. I write this to illustrate the number of conies around in those days and the work that was involved for the keepers of that time. I can't quote accurate figures but, on one particular estate, it was in excess of 30,000 bunnies in one year.

Ian said it was more difficult for the modern keeper on a rented shoot as it was essential to have good relations with the farmers, but that also applied on the large estates in the old days. The estate owners had a lot of power over the tenant farmers through their tenancy agreements etc. but it was the keeper on the ground who had to work with these farmers. Believe me, should one be crossed, he could be, and sometime was, most difficult, despite any agreements. You can't beat good relations between all country folk.

I hope you, the reader, enjoy my thoughts on the lives of modern and ancient keepers. I suppose it is inevitable that the modern keeper thinks he has a hard life, long hours and risky situations (with the modern poacher), but there are the compensations too, as there have always been. The pleasure of a good show of birds during the shooting season, and the knowledge of a job well done. As Ian said, let's agree to differ and get on with the job.

7 · JULY

HOW QUICKLY THE SUMMER PASSES. When July arrives, it is time to be thinking of checking the release pens, that is, if you have been successful and have some pheasant poults to release! There are a number of methods adopted to release poults. One is cutting the flight feathers on one wing and giving the young birds a fairly large wired-in area in which to settle down. It won't be long before the young birds have completed the moult and are able to fly over the wire netting. This method of release is very suitable on a small shoot, where birds have to be fed in hoppers and get only infrequent visits. If daily attention is available, a smaller release pen is probably more suitable. A wired enclosure of, say, 10 feet by 40 feet will accommodate up to 100 poults for a week or so. If these birds are gradually released, after a couple of days to settle down, they will remain close to the point where they were introduced to the wood. This type of pen must have a wire-netting roof and it is essential that the birds are fed regularly, if possible by hand and not by filling a hopper.

Whichever method is to be used, don't leave getting the pen or pens ready until the last minute. It really is best to do this job before any of the lush spring growth has reached the stage where working on the pens will flatten it. A nice bit of cover in the pens is very welcome to the poults when they arrive. After being handled, they suffer a certain amount of stress and, if they can get under cover for an hour or so, they

Young pheasants in a release pen in the wood.

seem to settle down much sooner. If the pen is naturally bare, a few branches (spruce is good for this) will provide hide for the poults.

Hopefully you have been spending a bit of time on your shoot this spring and, if so, you should have a good idea of the possibilities for a few wild birds. A dry, coldish period, on the face of it, should be a good omen, but this may not be the case. Most young game birds, and here

95

let's include ducklings, need a lot of insects for the first week or so. With dry weather, and in many places with frost at night, these insects would not be too abundant. But at least the young birds stand a better chance of survival than they would if there had been a very wet period immediately after being hatched. On a number of occasions, a period of thunderstorms and heavy rain has been known to wipe out the bulk of the young game birds. Partridges, despite the hen bird being a good mother, suffer during these wet spells, and a hen pheasant will lose practically all of her brood. A stupid bird in many ways, she will keep rambling on, despite the plaintiff *cheep-cheep* of her offspring trying to keep up in the wet grass. Soon these little balls of fluff are too weak to call the hen bird and eventually are left so far behind that they are lost and soon die.

Ducks are as a rule good mothers but have the rather unfortunate habit of starting to nest much too early in the year. The author once found a duck sitting on ten eggs very early in the year, in fact mid-January. There was little chance that that bird would rear a brood. Few ducks that hatch in the wild before early May have much chance to survive, as they need a large amount of insect life, which certainly is seldom available in April. The ducklings soon become weak and die. A mallard will have another go and nearly always is more successful at the second attempt.

Now what about the chances of a few wild birds on your particular shoot! It is very difficult, even for the professional gamekeeper, to be sure what success the wild birds have had. With a lot of growth in the woodland and hedgerow, there is plenty of 'hide' for any young birds but, come July, there is one pointer at least to how the pheasants have fared. Any chicks that have survived to the poult stage will now be in the process of moulting. By keeping an eye open for these small cast-off feathers, it is possible to get a rough idea what number of poults are about. A nice dry bank where the soil is exposed, a bare place at the base of a tree, or the edge of a cornfield are good places to look for evidence of young birds. They often cast their feathers, when 'dusting' so keep your eye on those sort of places and let's hope you find lots and lots of cast-off feathers. Don't confuse them with the old birds' cast-offs though!

Many shooting people may have seen a programme on BBC Nationwide about a poacher in Norfolk. This poacher claimed to have made a good living by poaching everything from rabbits, hens, partridges and pheasants to deer. He even included pigeon and snipe. He claimed 2000 pheasants a year on average, which he sold for £4,000! Now Norfolk, as everyone knows, is a good game county, and no doubt pheasants are abundant, but one man poaching on his own and not starting, as he said, until late November, would, in my view, be hard pressed to get this number of birds. Two hundred a week is a lot of pheasants and would, without others being involved, take a lot of disposing of. He seemed to pour scorn on the gamekeepers in his area, and there must be quite a lot, with so many pheasants around. He said 'Riding around in Land Rovers as they do these days, I always know where they are. If I go in a wood after pheasants and a pigeon flies out then I know it's safe'. Does he think that gamekeepers are stupid? A pigeon coming off the roost is one of many things a keeper is looking for! A great play was made of 'lamping' for rabbits and hares at night. Now this is one certain way, if you are poaching, of advertising your presence. The powerful beam needed from a torch to stupefy a 'bunny' can be seen nearly a mile away. Any keeper who misses such evidence is certainly not worth his salt, and no doubt any patrolling policeman would, particularly if he was a rural 'bobby', want to know what was going on.

The film of lamping rabbits was allegedly made on the property of a friendly landowner, the only 'friendly' one the poacher knew, the film said. This landowner, if he exists (the film was made at night don't forget), as a friend of the poacher, would appear to condone the poacher's claims. The film gave the impression that poaching was an easy and exciting way of making a good living. It must be hoped that if anyone watching fancied the idea, they forget it, for as sure as God made little apples, a keeper somewhere will catch them. Poaching is indeed a menace and goes on very often on an organised basis. Let's keep our fingers crossed that your particular shoot does not receive a visit from such a gang this coming winter.

The end of July brings the Game Fair. This is the opportunity to meet old friends and gather a few ideas. With so many people interested in all sorts of field sports, the Game Fair has become a very important date in the countryman's calendar. There is something for everyone, no matter what your favourite pastime may be, and in fact, with so much to see, it really needs the 3 days of the Fair to give one a chance to see it all.

*   *   *

Hopefully, by the time you are reading this, you will have some young pheasants feathering up nicely and, before long they will be ready to go to the wood. I wonder how many hours are spent throughout the rearing season, gazing at these young birds. As a gamekeeper, I would naturally spend some time observing the progress of my charges, checking for any sign of disease and hoping all would go well.

Many shooting people who rear a few for their own shoot must watch the growing chicks with differing thoughts. A picture no doubt comes to mind of later in the year; of some of those lively balls of fluff flying high, fast and handsome, out of a well-placed covert. A good many 'right and lefts' are visualised during a balmy summer evening at the rearing pens! Oh it's grand to dream, and even if some of the dreams don't come true, there is a lot of pleasure to be had just watching the progress of a pheasant from egg to release pen. But although it is right and proper to get pleasure from these visions, it must not blur the essentials, to provide the sport thus visualised.

I have already emphasised the advantage of getting the release pens ready in the woods in plenty of time, and the best way of releasing poults is at 6 or 7 weeks old. Many people in a small way may not have much option when it comes to this stage. A day is fixed and, no matter what, that is when the poults are moved to their new quarters. When people are following a full-time occupation and the shoot has to be attended to when time is available, the move has to be made no matter what the conditions. There is, however, no doubt that it is of great advantage to move poults when conditions are good. On a wet day, the poults are really unhappy. That is pretty obvious from their bedraggled appearance; with head down, and often drooping wings as well, it can be seen that a great deal of stress is being put on the unfortunate birds. No matter how carefully the poults are handled, and how nice the day, it is inevitable that a certain amount of stress will

98

occur, but handled on a wet day, with the handlers not too happy at being wet themselves, it is certain the stress will be severe. I have known more than one poult to suddenly die whilst a move was taking place under ideal conditions, which shows the considerable stress involved. Handle the birds with great care. Do not put too many in a moving box or basket; they are easily smothered. Don't stack too many containers on top of one another and, if possible, transport them in an open-topped vehicle. If you can release the poults on a dry, warmish day in a pen with at least some cover, and with the minimum of stress, your losses should be small.

Many a young pheasant is lost, often dying from pneumonia, because not enough care is taken when moving at the poult stage. If the poults are panting when you turn them out in the pen, it is more than likely that too many have been put in the container. In my experience, it is better to have a number of small boxes or baskets when moving birds, rather than one or two large hampers. In a large area, with many birds, there is a great risk of some being smothered or, failing that, becoming overheated and at risk from pneumonia. Watch the day, watch the handling, watch the size of containers, make sure the release pen is good and you should have a minimum of losses.

It is some time before the poults start to ramble, usually when they are 11 or 12 weeks old. In many cases, that is the time to start feeding them in woods or spinneys away from their 'home wood'. So far so good, but nobody wants the rambling to extend too far. Feed is the main factor that controls the movements of game birds and, as a rule, if feed is provided that the birds like, they will return to the feeding point.

I was talking recently to a gamekeeper friend, Brian Hatton, who is a very successful 'keeper' to boot. We were discussing the holding of pheasants in the coverts; not only in the right coverts, but in the right proportion. Professional gamekeepers (and Brian is that) like to have a larger number of birds in a wood that provides good sport (high flyers) than in a place that is inferior. It is a problem, particularly when the staff on a shoot is minimal, but Brian told me that he had tried a 'Pheasant Holding Block'. This is a block which consists of protein, oil, fibre and numerous additives and which is not a feed, but is

Keeper feeding young pheasants in a release pen in the wood.

particularly attractive to seed-eating birds. It appears that placing these blocks in the wood where you hope to have a nice lot of birds seems not only to hold those already there, but attracts some from the vicinity.

Being so attractive to seed-eating birds, numerous finches and the like may soon find out the delights of this block. Brian didn't mention any problems in this respect, and I must admit that it did not occur to me at the time of our conversation. I will bring the question up when we next meet. These blocks, are, I gather, quite reasonably priced and come in packs of two, weighing 20 kilograms in all. They last for quite some time, but may need to be turned at intervals of about a week, depending on the number of birds using them no doubt. They are available from Minsup Ltd of Winsford, Cheshire. A few blocks on an unkeepered shoot look quite an attractive proposition to me. I suggest you endeavour to keep them to the centre of your shoot. They may attract birds from over the boundary, but it is not a good idea to draw any of your precious stock away from the centre; they usually go too quickly anyway!

The British Association for Sport and Conservation are doing a good job around the country shows and country fairs this year, with their gun-handling lessons at the very reasonable fee of £3. I understand these lessons are aimed at the youngsters, the up-and-coming generation of sportsmen. With such a lethal weapon as the shotgun, the correct procedure of handling and use is essential. There is a right and a wrong way of doing everything and, when it comes to gun handling, there are quite a number of older folk I know who might learn something if they only watch!

*   *   *

There have been so many changes in the way of life in the country over the last half century, as much with country sports as with anything else, though the basic essentials are still there.

Thinking on these things recently, it was amazing the number of changes there have been, not all of them for the better. Today it is so often which is the easiest, and probably more important, which is the cheapest. These factors have had a big effect on the traditional things appertaining to field sports, but at the same time enabled many more people to enjoy them. In the past, it was hardly known for a working man to have the pleasure of shooting driven pheasants, for instance. Today many, probably thousands, do so. In the 1930s practically all the pheasant shooting was done on large estates, with many keepers employed, and an army of beaters on a shooting day. There was a correspondingly large bag, often 1,000 head was a poor day.

It wasn't just the number of keepers and beaters employed on these shoots, it was also the pageantry. On many estates, the beaters would be wearing white smocks, made of thick almost waterproof material, and decked out in real 'bush' hats. They gave a real splash of colour to the wintry scene.

The keepers would be in the livery of their employer, maybe green velvet jacket and waistcoat with brass buttons bearing the coat of arms, often white breeches and boxcloth leggings, and a hard hat emblazoned with gold braid; in all a marvellous sight.

The forgoing came to mind when thinking of the many changes, and thinking of July. July was the month when the keepers were measured for their new suits, for in those days most gamekeepers had a suit of clothes a year. It was not a velvet suit of clothes each year, for these were not suitable for the hard day-to-day work. Another suit of hard-wearing cord was more serviceable. The local tailor usually came to measure the keepers on the pheasant-rearing field, giving them plenty of time to make the suits (all hand-made of course) before the shooting season started. The keepers had to wear one of these suits at all times; I don't suppose many had a lounge suit to their name, having little need for one in fact.

Today (and this is one of the changes which, to me, doesn't appear be any great improvement), it is more likely to be a suit of plus fours every 2 years or so, and thus the keepers very often wear jeans or suchlike, except on shooting days. There is nothing wrong with plus fours or plus twos. They are a most suitable garment for most field conditions. It seems to me that a keeper in jeans cannot possibly have the same air of authority as one dressed in a plus-four suit. This may not seem important but when approaching a trespasser, who is maybe a poacher, it makes a lot of difference and, in my experience, commands a lot more respect. Maybe I am old and nostalgic! No matter, you will know from the 'ceremonial' keepers' dress of yesteryear, why men of that ilk were called 'old velveteens'.

Soon many pheasant poults will be going to the woods to greet the wide-open world after being confined to their breeding pens. This can be a very trying time with the risk of losses from predators in so many forms. Today, the poults are well-grown birds and soon go to roost, thus lessening the chance of Reynard getting amongst the 'jugging' birds at night.

Many years ago, I was involved in an experiment concerned with foxes. A number of pheasant poults were put in a small wood, which had the usual 6-foot wire netting around the perimeter, knowing that a litter of cubs had been reared nearby. The idea was based on the premise that a vixen rarely killed close to 'home' or where it was fed. In those days, foxes where often fed to keep them in an area for fox-hunting purposes.

Food for the foxes was put out each night. This was mainly rabbits, which were plentiful, or any dead poults that were available. Each morning almost all of the 'supper' had gone. This went on for a week or two, with no disturbance amongst the 'jugging' pheasants. Then one night, the feed which had been put out religiously night after night was ignored, a hole was scratched under the wire netting and quite a large number of young pheasants were killed!

The fact that a fox had been amongst them put the bulk of by now quite large birds up to roost and little further killing took place. It is difficult to know what this experiment proved, except maybe never trust Reynard! On the other hand, the old head-keeper who organised the job might have been craftier than it appears; if that litter of cubs hadn't been fed, perhaps they would have been in the wood more than once before the birds went to roost.

No, if you are taking birds to cover for release, don't bother to feed any foxes around. Much better to put an electric fence round the wood, making sure it is at the right height and with a fully-charged battery!

Despite the high cost of feeding game birds throughout the winter, quite a number of people do so. I'm not talking about in the woods,

A plastic bit on a young pheasant. The elasticity of the plastic allows the keeper to fit the bit quite easily but two pairs of hands are really needed to catch and hold the birds.

rather about the keeping of hen birds for the following year's egg production. This is obviously a wise move, so long as the expense of feeding is taken into account and the security of the pen is satisfactory (poachers have been known to empty such a pen before today).

With 6 or 7 week old birds it is quite easy to tell hen from cock and this is about the right time to select what stock you intend to keep. Before penning, the plastic bits used to prevent feather pecking must be removed. If the pen is small or overcrowded, the poults will sometimes start tail pulling. This makes the birds look rather unsightly, although only in extreme cases are there many losses.

I have mentioned 'Holding Blocks' for use in the wood. If these blocks are used in the pens of stock poults, tail pulling is greatly reduced and the poults mature much sooner. My suggestion is, try a feed block or two. I am sure you will be pleased with the results.

8 · AUGUST

THERE ARE FEW MORE PLEASING SIGHTS to the shooting man than a large number of well-grown pheasant poults feeding happily round a release pen in August. It's still a long way to go until October, or even November, but even late-hatched birds will soon be going to roost and be much safer from that ever-present taker of game, Reynard. Once the poults start roosting, and this is when they are about 9 weeks old, the chances of losses from predators are greatly reduced. Unfortunately, nature being what it is, a game bird is never completely safe and, despite every effort to protect them, losses will occur.

An old gamekeeper once said, after what had obviously been a period when his charges had suffered losses despite all his efforts 'I'm damned if I know why they call us gamekeepers, as far as I can see there's hardly a day goes by without we lose a head or two of game. "Gamelosers" would be more appropriate!' This keeper was a very successful and efficient producer of game, so any reader who should suffer a few losses amongst his released birds should not be too despondent. It happens to the professionals as well.

Very often, one of the greatest problems with released pheasant poults is rambling dogs. One on its own is bad enough, but should two get together they can, and will, do a terrific amount of damage in a very short while. Even farm dogs are not beyond sneaking off for a quiet bit of 'hunting'. Even though they may not kill many of the immature

Early training for the real thing: young labrador with pigeon in a wheatfield.

game birds, the fact that a disturbance is caused can drive the game away from its normal area, even onto an adjoining shoot. As long as young birds are able to get what feed they require, they tend to stay in that particular spot, so let's hope that your shoot does not have rambling dogs visiting it.

Farmers as a rule are pretty keen that no dogs should be hunting on their land, particularly if they have stock of any sort be it sheep or cattle. Even though you may live some way from your 'patch', you have an ally who will keep his eye on the problem of dogs.

A shoot with no footpaths criss-crossing the area is a rare thing. More people are using these paths today than did years ago. Most counties have these paths sign-posted, which is a good thing so long as the footpath doesn't run right through your best wood! Pamphlets and guide books are readily available to anyone wishing to take a country ramble in an area not familiar to them. Many of these publications give country walks for the motorist and it is only natural that there are more people taking advantage of the numerous rights of way, this is as it

106

should be, but one wonders at times whether the people who go to the trouble to motor out into the country are just taking a walk for the sake of walking or want to see the marvels of nature? Many of these people, obviously urban dwellers, wear such garish clothing that most birds and animals very soon decide to get out of sight. If ramblers wish to see the country wildlife, the way they dress tends to defeat the object. A number of people wearing brilliant orange or blue anoraks will upset any cattle in the fields which the rambler may cross. They are therefore not too popular with the farmers, let alone any person who may have game in the area. This clothing, which can be seen from such a great distance, is essential when walking in the mountains and high places of our delightful country as it does make rescue easier should a mishap occur, but please you ramblers who may read this, ask yourself the question, would you see more in dull clothing when walking the fields, riversides and streams?

Britain being a country of dog lovers, it is inevitable that when folk go walking in the country, they take their dog with them. This is only natural, but many of these dogs are not used to the wide open spaces and tend to run a bit wild, especially if there should be the scent of game. The damage these dogs can do is not realised by many of the people from the towns. Some no doubt think it great fun to see their Toby chasing a hare away into the distance. Maybe the Countryside Act of 1981 will bring the true facts home to them. It is to be hoped so.

In these modern days, with farmers employing much less labour, not many men work in the fields, so there is not the same chance of the erring ramblers being told of their attitude to walking in the country. A man on a tractor or other machinery is much less likely to see, or even bother to stop when he does see, say, a dog hunting along a hedge. It must, of course, be said that the vast majority of townsfolk who walk the country footpaths do care about the environment, and it is only right that these people should be made welcome by the rural dwellers. Many rambling clubs and associations do a good job, and ensure that their ramblers do follow the Country Code.

Shooting people co-operate when and wherever possible with these rambling clubs. It is much better to make it as easy as possible for ramblers to find their way across country, so why not ensure that any stiles, footbridges etc. are kept clear of undergrowth, and maybe that there is even a small sign or two giving the direction of the footpath. Most genuine country walkers carry maps, but a little help is always appreciated.

What has all this got to do with the shooting man you may say. Well, the easier it is for folks to find and follow the footpaths, the sooner they are away from your patch, thus causing less disturbance.

The more interest there is taken in this great countryside of ours, the better it will be for all concerned, be it walkers, fishermen, shooting folk, bird watchers or those who make a living off the land. It's a great heritage; let us look after it for future generations.

The grouse-shooting season is fast approaching. With the fluctuations over the last few years, some moors will be better than others as always, but what losses did the winter inflict on the stock of birds? Not having been in touch with moorland keepers for some time the information is not to hand, but a good long spell of decent weather in the early summer is a great help to any chicks hatched. Let's hope August turns out to be what it has always been called: 'Glorious!'

*   *   *

It is many years now since I first saw grouse shooting on the Ruabon moors of North Wales. In the early 1930s most moors were retained by their owners to entertain their relatives and friends at the beginning of the shooting season. Although good sport was always looked forward to, it was inevitable that some seasons did not come up to expectations, which was disappointing. Today many moors are run on a commercial basis and much can depend on the number of birds available, which can affect the number of days shooting and thereby the income from the moor.

It must be a worrying time for the persons managing these commercial moors when the early spring weather is not favourable for a good hatch and rearing season. The red grouse is a hardy inhabitant of our mountains, but the weather plays an important part when the breeding season arrives.

You might think that a cold wet spring would suit the mallard better, but here again, unless conditions are right, the number of

Heather burn pattern, indicating a typical cared-for grouse moor. There are small patches, working up to the natural firebreak of the road.

ducklings reared can be drastically reduced. With a heavy rainfall around the peak nesting season, many nests would be flooded out. Any ducklings that hatch have little chance of survival. They need a good supply of insects for a number of days after hatching and, although ducks are normally good mothers, the shortage of a supply of suitable food gives them little chance to rear the brood. Many ducks that have lost their eggs from flooding, or for that matter from any other means, will nest again, hopefully with more success.

These days, many large shoots with a lake or large expanse of water often rear quite large numbers of mallard. These birds can provide sport before the pheasant-shooting season starts. Under certain conditions, this can be good sport but the mallard, being a bird that so quickly becomes quite tame, is often difficult to put up off the water. Later in the season, when they have been shot at several times, the opposite applies and it can be difficult to get in position to get a shot! Of course, as time goes by, these tame, reared duck are joined by wild local and migratory birds and this improves the sport.

Fortunately, with modern rearing methods, adverse spring weather need have little effect on the production of good, healthy pheasant poults. Wet weather usually has a tendency to bring gapes with it but, although treatment is rather expensive, there is little reason to lose any of your precious birds from this once dreaded infestation. In the old days, most keepers had their own ideas about curing this problem but, on looking back on the things used, it is most doubtful if any of them were at all effective. One thing used was spirits of camphor. The idea was to add the camphor spirit to the drinking water during dry weather, when the poults would readily take it. If the dry spell lasted a few days, the birds would certainly look much improved, but other keepers who didn't use the spirit would tell you that their poults were much better as well. It would appear that the weather was a greater factor in the improvement than the medication. It is important to take action at the first sign of gapes. The best plan is to have the treatment for this infestation ready and waiting. When you need this type of thing in a hurry it is often not so easy to obtain and, even if only one or two birds are 'sneezing', it can soon spread through most of the poults and, should this happen, losses can be heavy indeed.

With the start of the shooting season on 12 August many dogs often put in a hard day's work, especially if walking up is the order of the day. Many dogs are largely taken for granted and are often family pets as well as 'field dogs'. It is certainly unfair to expect these animals to work hard over difficult terrain on the moor after a long period of lazing around the family home. How many people would like to run a marathon straight from a city desk? It is essential to give these faithful animals an extended period of exercise each day as the shooting season approaches. There is no short cut; it is a matter of taking the dog for longer periods of exercise each day for some time before going onto the moors to shoot. It has been estimated, that a dog going for a walk with its master, traces twice the distance, say 2 miles instead of 1 mile, so maybe a couple of miles covered by the person exercising would be enough; good for the dog and good for the master too!

Working on the moors in August is certainly a much different situation for a dog than working the low ground after pheasants in October or November. Yes, we know it can be quite cold, even in August, on the heather-clad moors, but when it is hot it is really tough going through deep heather and our foor-legged friend is loath to give up, even when gathering grouse behind a butt. Please give your dog some thought early in the season, a well-exercised, fit friend will enjoy his work so much more and be physically capable of doing it, and at the same time make your shooting days more enjoyable as well.

In previous chapters, I have mentioned one or two unusual incidents and, quite recently, a local gamekeeper was talking to me about such an occasion. He had been in the vicinity of the River Dee when he observed some activity from a couple of crows, which led him to think they were attacking something. When crows are hunting for eggs or other food they are as silent as an owl but, when mobbing a fox or a cat, their call can be heard a very long way. On further investigation, the keeper discovered that the pair of corvids were sweeping down onto the river, actually touching the water at times, and he soon found the reason for their frantic swooping – a moorhen with her brood! Of course, the young birds kept bobbing under the water when the crows struck but, in the end, the inevitable happened; one of the crows got a chick as it surfaced and the pair of black predators started to fall out over the prize. This lulled them into failing to see the gamekeeper and presented him with an easy right and left. Now at least some moorhens can cross the Dee in peace!

*   *   *

Once more the month when shooting commences is upon us. Sportsmen fortunate enough to be able to visit the grouse moors will be looking forward to that day of days, the 'Glorious Twelfth'. There is nothing like it. An August sun beating down on a vast expanse of heather in full bloom, moving dots in the far distance, and maybe a man or two much closer on the flanks who occasionally waves a flag. You know it won't be long before your skill with a gun will be called upon, with the sudden appearance of that fleeting target, the grouse. There can be few more exhilarating moments than that for the shooting man.

The moorkeeper will seldom say that birds are plentiful, for so many factors are involved. But as a rule he will know how the breeding season has gone and will have a pretty good idea what the bag should be, for so much depends on the ability of the sportsman to hit the target!

Early in the season, with the gun being in the gun cupboard for so many months, it takes a while to get the eye in, unless of course a session or two has been spent at clay pigeons. Some people say that shooting at clays does not help them at all when dealing with the real thing, but I suppose this really depends on the individual. A lot say that the average clay, when shot at, is starting to slow down, whereas the grouse puts on a spurt as soon as movement is seen in the butts. This is partly true. Many people have their clay shooting other than at a shooting school with a well-designed layout. A trap behind some bales of straw is bound to produce a slowing target. Though possibly providing a lot of fun, this is not going to greatly help someone practising for a day at driven grouse!

An hour or two at a shooting school, such as the one run by the Jones' brothers at Sealand, near Chester, will almost certainly improve the reaction and accuracy. This school, and many others up and down the country, have such a marvellous layout that almost any target likely to be found in the shooting field can be reproduced time and time again, and thus be of great help to the rusty sportsman.

It is to be hoped that the gun itself has been duly serviced during the off season. There is nothing more annoying than a gun failing to

Picker-up on grouse moor.

operate just when a nice covey of grouse are passing! This can so easily ruin the whole day, for even if another weapon is available to borrow, it is most unlikely that it will be the right fit, and it will probably lead to bruises on shoulders and cheek, or both. Perhaps it is too late to have a gun checked this season, at least for the grouse shooting, but it is well worth remembering for another year.

I wonder sometimes with the modern methods of rearing game whether keepers of the future will have the same knowledge of nature as those of my generation had to. I was standing talking to a young keeper a month or so ago, when a blackbird started piping just inside the wood. The lad took not a bit of notice, despite the fact that he was carrying a gun. To me this was a sure indication that a ground predator was afoot, may be a stoat or weasel, or even a rat or a cat. The blackbird was not agitated enough for it to be a fox on the prowl. Perhaps some readers are not aware of the warning notes of birds, for all birds give early warning to their brethren when danger is around. This piping note of the blackbird is best described as *pip-pip-pip*, usually with the bird in a bush or tree, casting a wary eye on the danger below. This call is used almost entirely for ground predators and another warning call *rit-tit-tit*, much like the call when going to roost, indicates winged predators: owl, jay, magpie etc. When the blackbird really gets agitated, both calls are sometimes used in conjunction for danger on the ground, a cat getting near a nest full of fledglings for instance.

I asked this young keeper 'Are you going?' 'Going where?' he replied, and so I had to point out the piping blackbird. By the time I had explained what it was all about, the 'blackie' had ceased so we never did know the reason for its distress. It is very difficult to describe the alarm notes of birds, but I did my best with the lad. No matter how poor my description, he should know when a blackbird has seen a stoat or the like! It seems a shame that the bright young lad didn't know of the indication of something afoot. Predators are not likely to be in a brooder house but, on the old open rearing field, it was a constant guard against the raids of vermin and this made it essential to know every indication of unwanted visitors.

Every bird has its alarm notes, in many cases more than one, and by long experience it is possible to know exactly what is going on. Where a bird has only one recognisable alarm note, to the human being that is, it is often possible to get a very good idea of the reason for the call by observing the situation from which the bird is calling, e.g. close to the ground – ground vermin, high in a tree – winged vermin. Only experience of these things can really give any degree of accuracy. In the old times, this knowledge of matters avian was essential, not only to know what vermin was afoot, for birds give evidence of human beings afoot too. Many years ago, an old keeper told me that he didn't have to go in a wood to know what was there. 'Sit on the fence and have a quiet pipe of baccy, lad. The birds will tell you all you want to know'. I found this quite true in later years. Providing it is not blowing a gale, listening for a while will give a very good indication of movement in the wood, human or otherwise. Just listen to the various birds and analyse their numerous calls.

I was with the same old keeper once whilst I was still a lad, when a blackbird came flashing down the track in the wood, giving its winged-predator call after flying straight out of a large privet bush. I grabbed for the gun, but the old keeper said 'Come on behind this bush quick, taint no hawk, more likely a man'. Sure enough, shortly afterwards, a woodsman came strolling down the wood and walked straight past us, without casting an eye in our direction.

I can only hope that my chat with the young keeper taught him as much as when that old keeper said to me when the woodsman had gone 'Out a bush, hide; in a bush, dive' (for your gun).

9 · SEPTEMBER

GROUSE SHOOTING, as has been said so many times, is the most exhilarating and testing of all shooting. The gently sloping moorland, with its craggy outcrops and valleys with the bubbling (or should it be 'babbling') brooks, make a wonderful backcloth for that highly-prized target, the red grouse. Over the years there have been many changes to the grouse-shooting scene. It was rare indeed in pre-war days for anyone other than members of the aristocracy to be able to have a day on the moors. In modern times, so long as the person can afford to pay the naturally high charges, it is possible to have a day's grouse shooting. Even some rough shoots in the valleys of Wales have a small area of heather on the higher parts and it is not unknown for the odd grouse to put in an appearance there, usually when the grouse moors in the area have been shot over a number of times.

It is obviously not worth the tenants of these rough shoots to make a special foray after grouse, but sometimes the odd bird is picked up if any particular shoot should be fortunate enough to have some partridge on it! Partridge seem to be on the increase in some places but, even if your shoot has a covey or two on it, don't be too heavy on them. A short day in September is about the most you can expect, but what a pleasant day that can be. It is doubtful that you will have enough partridges to warrant having a drive or two but by walking them up you will get plenty of exercise and fresh air and maybe a plump bird or two to make a tasty meal.

Walking up grouse; a bird jumps up.

If a walking day is arranged it is advisable to ask tactfully any guns or helpers taking part who have a 'wild' dog to leave it at home! There is nothing more annoying or frustrating than a wide-ranging dog putting up a nice covey of partridges just out of gunshot! You may have to walk half a mile before you catch up with the covey and they will be pretty alert by then. It won't need a dog to put them into the air, more likely a lot of stealth to get anywhere near them. Once you find a covey, don't follow it up until almost the last bird has been accounted for. There is a lot of natural winter wastage with partridge, so go lightly with any birds you may be fortunate enough to have on your patch. With a bit of luck there may be some for another year.

By September, all the pheasant poults should be in the woods, thriving on their freedom. It won't be long before they start to explore the area surrounding their home cover and this is really a rather critical time. If the shoot is not very large, they can soon be over the boundary. It is unfortunately all too common for rather unscrupulous people to take advantage of this and feed the rambling birds. The only thing that can be done by non-resident shooting folk is to make sure the fast-growing poults are never short of food and water – and don't forget the grit. Even then they can stray some considerable distance.

It is essential to know the movements of your birds if you want a good shooting season. By knowing which spots they favour, it is possible to ensure that too many don't go over the boundary. Hard feeding every day is the best way, so by putting feed hoppers and water containers of one sort or another in these favourite spots, most birds will keep returning. It is not advisable to put these feed hoppers too close to the boundary but, if you have a wood or spinney that runs up to the limits of your shoot, make sure the birds have feed available. Do not put the feed hoppers out until you are pretty certain some of the tame birds have arrived in that area; this should then create a 'holding' situation. If the feed is available too soon, it may create a 'drawstring' situation and you may find a lot more birds in that spot than you would wish. In any case, it is essential, especially on a small shoot, to keep reared birds in or near the home cover as long as possible; they will spread out soon enough!

What about the ducks? If there are a lot of ducks on your shoot and you have also reared some, you will no doubt want to have an hour or two after them in September. Years ago, before the advent of the combine harvester, a lot of fun was had flighting duck coming into the stubbles to feed at dusk. With the binder, the sheaves of corn were set up into stooks and left out in the fields for, as the old farmers said 'the church bells to ring over them thrice'. This method of harvesting inevitably meant a large amount of grain was shed and thus there was plenty of feed for the ever-hungry mallard. Today's harvesting of grain does not leave a lot of feed behind for any kind of wildlife, but it is still possible to get one or two ducks under the right circumstances. Most wheat and barley grown these days is of the short-strawed variety; thus there is much less chance of it being laid by wind and rain but, nevertheless, there are often patches that don't do so well, having maybe a small area of earth showing. These are the spots the ducks will find and, of course, any areas that may have been flattened by extreme weather conditions.

Pre-war, the stooks of corn made ideal hides for duck flighting;

today use has to be made of any available cover. It is not necessary to be out in the middle of the corn; once the flight line has been ascertained, quite good shooting can be had from a surrounding hedge. Mallard will probably give better sport from outside the corn where they will be quite a bit higher! A little information is needed before setting out on such an expedition. The farmer is the man most likely to provide this and, no doubt, will be only too pleased to do so. It is amazing how much damage to a crop a large number of feeding duck can do, let alone the Canada goose, should there be any in the area.

It is not advisable to go flighting too often. After the first visit the mallard will be very loath to settle in to feed once they have heard a shot and they will take off for pastures new! It is often almost dark before these disturbed birds come back, so should you wait for them, have a good dog available to retrieve any ducks that may be wounded. A dog is essential in any case. You won't be too popular if you trample up and down the standing corn a dozen times or so!

If you have reared and released some duck and put a ring on them, you will know if your reared ducks are stubble feeding should you kill any, but it is much the best to leave the reared duck in peace. They don't normally go far from their pond if well fed. When pheasant shooting starts you can have some fun with them as described earlier.

*   *   *

September always brings back memories of partridge shooting. Gone are the days when the corn was cut by a binder and the sheaves set up in stooks for the grain to ripen, a rural scene the younger generation can only see in photos or paintings. Many farms were quite small compared to modern times and the fields were smaller too, but what a delightful sight it was to see the patchwork of fields with the corn waiting to be carried and put into stacks, until the threshing machine could produce the by then hardened grain.

These fields were a haven for the partridge coveys, which were little affected by the slower, quieter farming activities. With the patchwork of corn fields, if work was going on in one, only a short distance away another would be free of disturbance.

The little brown bird loved all the insects that were so plentiful in

Partridge shoot, Hampshire, 1956.

the stooks of corn and, of course, the grain itself, which was so easy to feed on.

Even away from the well-known partridge areas, many places carried quite a stock of birds. With the coming of September, small shooting parties would be organised, often with several farmers joining forces, for a most enjoyable day's sport. As a rule, these days were spent walking up the partridges. Where there were root crops – turnips, mangolds and potatoes – the trick was to walk the stubble field first, always driving the coveys into the roots. Once the birds were in the thicker cover of the roots, much sport could be had by walking in line as slowly as possible, usually putting the coveys up well in range of the sportsmen.

On occasions, guns would stand so that the disturbed birds were driven over them; in effect they were driven birds, but mostly these small shooting parties preferred not to take too heavy a toll of their stock of partridge and only walked them up.

This was part of rural life before the last war, but with the modern farming methods with large fields (the pulled-up hedges have reduced the nesting sites), large and fast moving machines, and the stubble either burnt or ploughed up within days, there is not much chance of those delightful days spent after the partridge returning, more's the pity.

Perhaps I am a bit critical about the farming methods of today. Farming has to be viable but sometimes things seem to have gone a bit too far, and so much of the activity is detrimental to the wild life of this pleasant land of ours. There seems to be a change in the air and let's hope more people will come to realise what is at stake. It is not only the shooting people who stand to lose!

I recently experienced one of the most severe thunderstorms that I can remember. The rain was torrential but worst of all were the large hailstones – well hardly hailstones, lumps of ice would be more accurate – causing a vast amount of damage to greenhouses and gardens. Broad beans and cabbage were devastated and the large rhubarb leaves were torn to shreds, and even the rhubarb sticks were cut in half by the vicious onslaught of the falling 'ice'.

This freak of nature is mentioned for one reason: what damage would such a storm do to young pheasant and partridge chicks out in the field? Probably the partridge would fare better than the pheasant, so long as the brood was on fairly high ground when the storm struck. The hen is a good mother and would not desert her brood, but with such a heavy fall of water in a short period, should the brood have been on low lying ground, the flooding would give no chance of survival for the chicks.

I remember once in Norfolk, a fair number of years ago now, when a similar storm struck (less the hailstones) and the ditches and watercourses were literally full of drowned partridge chicks.

No doubt the pheasants would come off worse in such a storm. A notoriously bad mother, the hen pheasant would, without a shadow of doubt, soon be seeking cover, leaving the chicks to follow as best they could. They would have no chance in such a storm. Some of the earlier-hatched birds, being stronger, may have survived but I wouldn't give anything under a month old any chance in such a devastating 'unnatural' occurrence.

Some of the lumps of ice came down with such force that many greenhouses lost most of the glass and even some cars received quite sizeable dents, so it makes one wonder what a direct hit on a small chick would do. There can only be one answer: kill it. In that combination of water and falling ice, many wild game birds must have suffered heavy losses.

September is the month when hand-reared pheasants start to ramble away from the home covert, so it is well worth while to spend as much time on your shoot as possible. Conditions will dictate whether you can do anything about it or not, but at least you will know where the birds are heading and some action may be possible. Turning them back towards the home will help if they haven't been going that way for long, but don't create too much disturbance or some birds will be lost and thus you defeat your object.

As has been said before, feed is the controlling factor. September is a good time to assess where feeding hoppers may be needed. Often the same spot year after year is suitable but, with changing conditions, e.g. farm crops, a fresh place may well be more appropriate.

Keep your eye on the fast-growing poults, feed them well and in the right place and you should enjoy the fruits of your labour.

*   *   *

Many people will be looking forward to their first season shooting, for it is remarkable how many folk are clamouring to get some sport. It is not easy these days to join an established syndicate and, even if the opportunity does arrive, it is often too expensive for the average pocket. The sportsman or woman who has been lucky and managed a gun or half gun in a syndicate should only expect sport in proportion to the amount paid.

A small shoot relying on some wild birds will be comparatively cheap, but large bags cannot be expected. A fair stock of birds must be left for another year and it would be very unfair on a keeper, if one is employed, to do otherwise.

A large shoot employing a keeper and maybe a lad as well is bound to be pretty pricey, but as a rule is good value for money. A large part of the contribution of each member of the syndicate has to go in wages, housing and essential transport, so only part of the total can be used for rearing purposes. With the price of feed for game birds, it is inevitable that the number of reared game is tied to the amount each gun pays.

It is difficult to put a figure on what, say, each pheasant costs to rear up to the shooting season, for so much depends on so many factors. £1,000 won't go all that far, that's for sure!

I write this deliberately, for some people starting their first season shooting expect more than they can possibly get for their money. I say, enjoy the countryside, enjoy the company and enjoy whatever sport comes your way, whether it be partridge, pheasant or duck. At the end of the season, be grateful for your pleasure, and not critical of those taking part, for practically all are there for the enjoyment.

The milk quota applied to farmers may seem a queer thing to write about in a book such as this but, since its introduction, many farmers in the milk production business will have to reduce their stock of cows. This is where it may affect the sporting side of the country, depending on what the farmers turn to to offset their loss of income from milk.

Should the growing of cereals become more popular in what is normally a grassland area, it should in theory be helpful to the game population, but not necessarily to some people interested in game. Say, for instance, there is a nice little shoot at present surrounded by large tracts of grass fields and then a fair area is turned over to the plough to grow an arable crop. It is almost certain that the arable crop will attract game from a preserved shoot. Should there be nice warm woods with good roosting, that is where the pheasants will stop. If there is a possibility of this happening, it might be a good idea to ensure friendly relations with the farmers concerned and, who knows, you may eventually even be able to shoot over that area.

The quota is of great financial concern to the farmer but could also be of some concern to the shooting tenant. Farmers are a bit unpredictable and it is anyone's guess what they will do under the circumstances. There are many rumours of what 'old so-and-so' will do. I even heard one rumour that a certain farmer was intending to grow 50 acres of strawberries! Should encourage a few partridges!

A lot of shooting people will be looking forward to 1 September, if not for the partridge shooting, then for the duck shooting, both of which start on the same day.

There are many thousands of members of Wildfowling Clubs dotted all over the country, and these days most clubs have long waiting lists as there are so many wanting to join. It is most pleasing to know that these clubs have very strict rules. Woe betide a member who does not abide by them. In most cases it means being banned from the club, and probably any other club as well.

Gone are the days when any Tom, Dick or Harry could go on the marshes and get large bags of wildfowl. Most estuary marshes are either rented or under the control of the Wildfowling Clubs, and these

Wildfowler, 1934.

clubs run an efficient warden service to deal with any 'cowboys', or should it be 'gunmen', who may be operating to the detriment of the wildfowl stocks.

Most club members are quite satisfied to go on the marsh, to have only two or three shots, and to return home with an empty bag, muddy but happy. Just seeing the ducks, of many varieties, makes the trek worth while. I am sure there are many club members who do not bag more than three or four mallard during the whole season. It is very pleasant on those vast muddy flats on a fine September morning or evening, but there is not so much in the way of wildfowl about, none of the migratory birds having arrived. It takes a dedicated wildfowler to face the rigours of winter, with ice in the creeks, a force eight gale, and flurries of snow, but there are plenty of this tough hardy breed around!

Many clubs rear quite large numbers of mallard for release on inland waters. These birds are often ringed and quite a number are accounted for when they fly to the estuaries. It is good to see people putting back as much, or more, than they take out of their sport.

At a Wildfowlers' Club annual dinner earlier in the year, it was most encouraging to see quite a good sprinkling of young members present, for wildfowling is really a sport for the young and, with the continued interest of younger sportsmen, it is a good omen not only for the wildfowl of our country but for conservation in general.

10 · OCTOBER

NTICIPATION IS ONE OF THE GREAT PLEASURES of the shooting man. If October brings nothing else, it brings anticipation to all who have lavished so much care and attention on rearing pheasants, and perhaps reference to money should be added to the care and attention.

It never has been cheap to rear game birds and, these days, the cost seems to escalate from year to year. It is perfectly natural that those who rear pheasants in a small way should have this sense of anticipation, probably more so than a landed gentleman who can afford to employ a gamekeeper or two!

Even late-hatched pheasants will be getting into good big birds by now and, no doubt, eating their heads off. Many shooting men like to start their pheasant shooting this month but, by and large, few pheasants are ready to shoot until very late on in the month.

It is so pleasant to be out and about in the countryside in October, with all the changing hues of the foliage, but the very fact that most trees are still well 'clothed' should make a pheasant shooter hesitate to organise a day's shooting. If the trees still have plenty of leaves on them, there is sure to be pretty dense undergrowth as well and these conditions are not conducive to good sporting shots. Wait until the birds are really mature, not just fully feathered, and by then the undergrowth will be less and there will not be such a dense canopy above. The pheasants can then rise and fly high, so giving a much more

Pheasant shoot, Droitwich, 1935.

sporting shot, which is what, hopefully, they were reared for.

I have already given a number of tips or hints on the best methods of organising a day's shooting on a small syndicate or rough shoot. There is no need to go into these matters again, but it is certainly worth mentioning the importance of safety – meaning gun handling. On one large keepered shoot known to the author, when the guns have

126

assembled (in this instance at the owner's house), a short lecture is given by the host to all the guests present. He always greets his friends and guests with a cheery 'Good morning, gentlemen' and then proceeds to tell them which 'drives' are scheduled for the day's sport and this is followed by an emphasis on the need for gun safety. 'At no time gentlemen, will you walk with a loaded gun (there are no "walking" guns on this particular shoot). Guns will not be loaded until the whistle is blown to start the drive and, when a double blast of the whistle is heard, guns will immediately be unloaded. Between whistle, guns will always be in the "broken" position. Those are my instructions gentlemen, may you all have a good day's sport.' This particular gentleman was perhaps a bit of a martinet when it came to the shooting field but, nevertheless, well loved by all, despite the fact that the foregoing lecture had been delivered to some of the guns maybe scores of times!

At the recent Game Fair, there seemed to be much more concern about conservation, shown both by the number of displays and by the people to whom I had an opportunity to speak. This subject of conservation has inevitably to cover a very large spectrum of rural life. Many people have their own ideas about it, mostly quite naturally on how it affects them. However, if enough people show sufficient concern, it must in the end have its effect, and there are many signs of changes for the better evident today.

Although not what many people would call 'conservation', the following incident, or should it be incidents, gave me plenty of room for thought. Whilst in a different part of the country recently for a short visit, something that must be repeated thousands of times a day throughout the land was enacted. The people with whom the writer was a guest had recently acquired a black kitten about 9 months old. This kitten had the run of the house and, of course, the run of the garden, and no doubt many of the adjoining gardens as well. A small window was left open at night so that access was available to its favourite cushion, its bowl of milk and dish of tinned cat food. This milk and food was available to the feline 24 hours a day.

On the first morning of my stay, on entering the kitchen looking for a cup of tea, there was the kitten playing with the remains of a chaffinch. On remarking to the hostess that 'Tom' had brought a bird into the house she replied 'Oh Tom's a good cat. He brings one or two in every day'. Right enough, after staying 10 days, the number of birds Tom had brought into the house totalled fifteen plus one mouse (house). Several varieties of birds had been killed: thrush, blackbird, sparrow, chaffinch and blue tit, some young and some old. Now with literally thousands of kittens and cats throughout the land, what havoc this must make amongst the small bird population.

Not all cats are hunters to this extent, there can be no doubt about that, but if only a third of all the cats kill one bird a day, what a staggering total it must make. The writer then thought of the anti-blood-sports people and wondered how many of them kept a 'Tiddles' as a pet. No doubt a very large number of them do but it is a mistake to think that well-fed cats will not kill anything as the Tom which this item is written about proves.

A tax on cats would no doubt be impossible to operate but I wish there were many less moggies in the land, particularly in the rural areas where a cat which has 'gone wild' will take a lot of wildlife. It is doubtful though, if these feral cats kill just for the sake of killing, as so many of those well-fed pets of urban areas do!

*   *   *

By October, most of the crops will have been harvested and many fields will, weather permitting, already have been ploughed and sown with winter wheat or barley. In pre-war days, very little winter grain was sown and so there was no urgency to plough the stubble. This was beneficial to the game birds. Spraying crops was almost unheard of and so the stubbles held myriads of insect life and not a few weeds.

What a sight it was to see hundreds of reared pheasants ranging these stubbles in search of insects and the grain shed during harvesting operations. Most keepers were happy when there was a stubble field or two close to the home cover. It often saved them a lot of work driving the birds back home and probably reduced the employers' feed bills by a few pounds!

Today, with the land being ploughed and sown with 'dressed grain' so quickly after the combine harvesters have finished, plus the heavy use of insecticides etc., there is very little 'natural' feed for the game birds, wild or reared.

On an unkeepered shoot, this could possibly be an asset. The pheasant cannot be seen so easily (less information for the poaching fraternity) and relying on food provided in hoppers gives a bit more control over where the birds will be. Talking about hoppers, don't get the idea that you can attract pheasants to any position you want by putting a feed hopper there. It is true that some birds are sure to visit this source of feed but, unless the environment is suitable, they are unlikely to stay in the vicinity for long. As I have said before, you must make sure your feed point is in a spot which game birds favour. This spot may not necessarily be a good spot to shoot the birds, but it is surprising how far birds can be taken by careful driving before they are put over the waiting guns on a shooting day.

Dogs play a very large part in a good day's sport, be it grouse, duck, partridge or pheasant shooting and, come to that, pigeon shooting as well!

Over the years, I have seen many really top-class dogs but I must admit most of them were being used to 'pick up' after a pheasant shoot. The average shooter these days needs a dog with qualities rather different from those employed solely for retrieving the dead and wounded after a pheasant drive.

On the large keepered shoots, dogs may not be used at all for flushing the birds; the number of birds involved prevents this. A rather wide-ranging dog can so easily flush a large number of birds at once, something a keeper rarely wants. On some shoots (usually commercial ones) where a bag limit is fixed for the day, it is sometimes the keeper's ploy to send a large number of birds over the guns in one 'flush'. This keeps the bag down a bit, otherwise the allotted total might be reached by lunchtime, which is not a good thing when the guns are paying good money for a day's sport. This large flush can be much better controlled without dogs in the wood. Sometimes, where ground cover is sparse and the birds are in large numbers, the very sight of a dog will make them uneasy and they are not long before they erupt in one large flush.

There must be a very large number of the shooting fraternity who get as much pleasure out of working their dogs as out of the actual shooting but, of course, unless the dog is reasonably well trained, there can be much frustration too. This brings to mind one incident on a small syndicate shoot where a few reared pheasants were released and the woods had dense undergrowth. Each member was expected to bring a dog to work this 'jungle' as no beaters could be afforded. At the start of one season, one of the guns had a young dog with which he had been working hard all summer to make steady and obedient. All went well on the first drive but, during the second, 'Sam' failed to respond to any of his owner's calls and, when the party reached the end of the wood, the dog was nowhere to be seen. No-one had set eyes on Sam since the start of the drive and the luckless owner was very concerned as to the dog's whereabouts. As the party was about to move off, one member noticed sheep moving on a distant hill (the shoot was in Wales) and, lo and behold, the wayward Sam could be seen rounding up the sheep like a sheep dog. The frustrated owner had to go and collect his dog, which was kept on a lead for the rest of the day, completely spoiling his master's enjoyment of the sport. Needless to say, this dog did not appear on the shoot again and became a pet rather than a working dog.

Training a dog properly is a skilful job and needs a lot of patience and know-how. Many books are available on this subject but probably the most important thing is getting to know the dog's temperament and, believe me, they are all different. Pups can be sent to dog trainers. There are quite a number about, and most of them excellent men and women, but when the subject comes back from what will inevitably be an expensive training period, it is essential to ensure that the standard achieved is maintained. Many dogs, on returning from the trainer, are often allowed to slip back into their old ways and thus good money and time has been wasted.

There is probably nothing more satisfying to the true sportsman than working a dog you have trained yourself, even if you aren't shooting, and often large shoots need good dog handlers to pick up on a shooting day. 'Picking up' is, in its way, a skilful job. I have seen 'dog men' standing 20 yards behind the guns and, when the 'rise' is over, using their dogs to retrieve the dead birds around them. Quite

A good head-up delivery to the picker-up.

unnecessary. Dead birds can easily be picked up in this situation by the beaters or the gun himself. The dog man's place is a long long way behind the guns, in a position to see any wounded birds that may fall a couple of hundred yards from where they were shot and, being in a spot to mark where they fall, save the bird suffering and help the bag as well. The man who likes to work his dog amongst the guns and stand so that he can see the quality of the shooting (sometimes passing adverse comments) is less likely to be asked to that shoot again than the man who is out of sight but eventually appears laden with birds that would otherwise have been lost.

I will finish with a story which was told in the village pub one evening and, knowing the man who told it, I am sure the facts are true.

Alec Minshull, a good friend and a great dog lover (and for that matter handler), had, during the very hot spell, been in the habit of taking his two labradors for a swim in a pond close to his house. Of course, they looked forward to this outing and were always eager to get into the water. Alec usually kept them to heel until he could see that there was no wildlife on the pond for them to disturb but, this particular evening, he sent them on before reaching the pond. When Alec got there, he thought the oldest of the pair was in trouble. It was about 4 yards out on the surface of the water with its eyes shut and barely any movement from its outstretched legs. Alec called and straight away 'Trout' started to swim for the bank.

This raises the question, can or do dogs on occasion 'float'? After a lot of discussion no conclusion was reached, I will leave it at that, but Trout must have that ability!

*　　*　　*

After a hot dry summer most of the corn crops should have been harvested in good time. Combines make such a difference these days and, given good weather, a large acreage can be cleared in a short while. These factors will have been helpful to the fox hunts, for once the corn crops have been cleared, cub hunting can commence. Cub hunting is an essential part of country sport and for that matter country life.

At one time, the main object of cubbing was to break up the litters of cubs and disperse them over a wider area, ready for the more serious business of hunting proper. There was little emphasis on the kill. Today, with so many foxes in the country, particularly in urban areas, a lot more cubs are killed during the cubbing season. In most areas, there are plenty more to fill up any vacuum created.

Hunting and shooting people have not always seen eye to eye, though there are many who both hunt and shoot. The shooting man does not mind cubbing so much, for very few of his reared pheasants have left the home covert whilst cubbing is taking place. Most woods in which pheasants are released are wired round and little disturbance is caused. When it comes to the actual hunting of foxes, usually starting in November, it is a different kettle of fish. The game birds are well distributed and shooting, if not already taking place, is about to start. No one wants them disturbed. Some areas, particularly well wooded ones, are not affected so much as a shoot where small woods are some distance apart.

The hunting people have always maintained that after a pack of hounds had been through the woods the pheasants would fly better.

132

Very true, but in so many cases there weren't so many to fly better!

Today with so much pressure being put on country sports by the anti-blood-sports groups, there are signs that the hunting and shooting people are getting together to present a united front to this threat. It is possible, with good will between the hunters and shooters, for both to enjoy good sport. The hunt must be prepared to organise their days so that the minimum of disturbance is caused to game; even, if necessary, having their day after Reynard in an area which may be not quite so good from the hunting angle. At the same time, the shooting man must compromise and allow the hunt to draw his game coverts after, say, the second shoot. After a couple of days shooting, the numbers have been thinned out and any that are going to leave the area will have done so.

Just one more point, there must be liaison between the two parties so that the hounds don't meet too close when a shoot is scheduled. I don't know of anything more frustrating than a pack of hounds running through a wood just as a drive is about to commence! Please work together for the sake of country sport in general. Without genuine co-operation, the 'antis' will seize the chance, and make capital out of it.

South Buckinghamshire hounds at North Ufton, 1930s.

October means the pheasants are practically full grown and are eating their heads off, an expensive business, no matter what the feed. However well these birds are fed, many of them will want to seek pastures new. In the old days, the keepers used to use a lot of cut wheat and fine maize grit incorporated in the feed. This, well scattered in straw litter, made the birds scratch around and, in general, work harder before they had a crop full. Today, most game birds are fed on pelleted feed until large enough, then wheat, a much cheaper feed, is the main diet. The 'Pheasant Holding Blocks' mentioned in Chapter 7 will not keep the feed bill down, but if they only make a small percentage of birds stay at home instead of straying over the boundary, they must be a good investment.

Washing a motor car can hardly be called a job to give one inspiration but, after a long evening journey recently, my car was badly in need of a wash. Despite frequent use of the windscreen washers and wipers there were many squashed flies, moths and other insects.

Standing looking at this mass of dead insects, it dawned on me that there must be literally millions of these killed every day and night. With so many cars on the road, there must be a very heavy toll of the above and I wondered what effect this would have on other wildlife. When you come to think of it, it is not only that these insects are killed, but their breeding potential is lost. Will some of these, and there were quite a number of moths amongst the casualties, become rare or even eventually extinct?

Man, so often seeking to improve his living conditions, does not fully realise the damage he is doing to wildlife. I think we must include the motor car in the list of wildlife destroyers. Anyone making even a short journey in a motor car is almost sure to see the remains of both birds and mammals by the side of the road. These casualties range from foxes, badgers (and I wouldn't like to hit a badger at 50 miles an hour) to stoats, weasels and mice, and birds from pheasants downwards. It must be a massive total countrywide, one that can never be arrived at and perhaps, for the peace of mind of us country lovers, this is just as well.

I must add though, be very careful should you try to avoid a bird or animal on the roads. With the speed of modern traffic, an accident is so easily caused. At the same time, don't deliberately run over anything. I have seen motorists swerve from side to side not to avoid, but to hit, a pheasant. On one occasion with dire results – the motorist went through a hedge!

11 · NOVEMBER

IT'S AMAZING HOW SOON the shooting season passes. After months of work during the spring and summer, November is upon us, and really it is only a matter of weeks before game shooting comes to an end once again. The best must be made of every week of the shooting season, and not necessarily by shooting your 'patch' every week. This is not a good thing at all unless you have a vast acreage and plenty of ground cover, which can make it possible to use the same area every 3 weeks or so.

Many rough shooters, and for that matter syndicates, do shoot over their piece of ground every week, mostly on a Saturday. It would be much better if a few days during the season could be left blank. Surely it would be possible for the members of a shoot to assist in one way or another on some other syndicate in the vicinity, even maybe to be invited to shoot as a guest. This arrangement could naturally be reciprocated and, although more than one other shoot might be involved, and it would take a bit of working out, it could only be to the advantage of all concerned.

Shooting people who become members of syndicates, whether they be keepered or not, and expect to be shooting at least once a week and, in some cases, expect to kill as many pheasants as poults released at 6 weeks, should not, in my opinion, be shooting game at all. It would be better if they stuck to clays! Some shoots are bound to do better than others. Much depends on so many factors: the type of country, the labour put in and, not by a long way the least, what sort of breeding season there has been. With a good stock of birds left at the end of the shooting season, good predator control and the right sort of weather at the right time, and if the area is suitable for game, it may be possible for the total bag at the end of the season to be close to the number of poults released but it is much more likely to be around 40 per cent or even less.

Should this be the first season you have released birds on a newly-acquired shoot, don't be despondent if the returns are not as you had hoped. It often takes a season or two to build up the stock on new ground and you also have to get to know how to shoot the area to the best advantage.

Some of the most sought after rough shoots are those close to a large estate where thousands of pheasants are released every year. It is inevitable in this sort of situation that some of the estate birds will ramble on to the rough shoot, particularly if there is feed put down to attract them. Don't, please, set out deliberately to attract these birds. A gamekeeper has enough to contend with without someone just over his boundary trying to get his charges to feed on their patch. Some will arrive without being drawn by feed and if, as in so many cases, you are not rearing birds of your own, be grateful for the few birds that arrive of their own volition.

Many estates these days wing-tag their pheasants; one reason for this is to find out how far they ramble and in which direction they tend to go. These tags are of different colours and numbered, so should you find any on birds killed on your shoot, it would be of great help to let any large shoot in the area know where you had killed the particular bird and whether it was a cock or a hen. Better still why not call on the keeper and have a chat! Much better to be friendly with the keeper on a nearby shoot – who knows what may come of it.

Talking of killing game, many people are in some doubt how to tell an old bird from a young one. Of course, a young bird is more succulent than an old one but many game birds will sometimes live to a fair age. In grouse, the first game bird to be shot, the young are usually picked out by the glossy plumage, with the spurs undeveloped and the quill feathers loose. With the partridge, the young are mainly

Wing-tagging a young pheasant.

distinguished by the legs being yellowish, but perhaps the most important sign of a young bird is that the longest wing feathers are sharply pointed. In an old bird, the long feathers are rounded. Ducks and geese show much the same characteristics in the young birds. The young normally have pliable and easily-broken yellow bills and supple yellow feet. Young pheasants should have bright plumage and smooth legs, with the cock birds having short spurs. None of these factors are infallible and should only be taken as a guide. Sometimes a very old pheasant will have short spurs, and sometimes a young one will have spurs that are well developed. With a cock pheasant the writer prefers the 'tail method' of telling young from old. Most second-season cock pheasants have longer tails than young birds, and not only longer tails but forked ones, much like a swallow's. This 'forking' of the tail is almost a 100 per cent indication of an old bird.

With rabbits and hares, it is quite easy to tell the young from the old; in both cases the bottom jaw is very easily broken in the young ones.

The foregoing is given as a pretty good guide to the age of game

138

birds, but it still takes some experience to sort out the young from the old. Naturally, most gamekeepers become pretty good and accurate at doing so. Nevertheless, the writer recalls one incident that happened many years ago and involved a goose and a certain head forester. The head forester had never tasted a wild goose and, at the appropriate time of the year, asked a gamekeeper on the estate to try to get one for him. Quite a lot of white fronts visited the water meadows at that time. The keeper in due course paid a visit to the meadows and managed to shoot a goose. He wasn't too worried about it being young or old; it was a goose for Sandy, the head forester! He took the goose to the head-forester's house and Sandy was delighted and gave the keeper a drop of scotch, and told him he would get it plucked and dressed and hang it for a week or so with an onion in it. Sometime later the keeper met Sandy and asked him what the goose was like, whereupon he got the reply 'Ach laddie, dinna talk to me about geese, it was that tough, we couldn't chew the gravy'.

Hoping all the game you choose is tender and good, but please don't blame me if its tough!

*   *   *

November is the month in which most pheasants are shot. These days, shooting certainly starts much earlier than pre-war but nevertheless, when the leaves are off the trees, much better sport is obtained and few of the large estates will start any of their 'big' days before then.

The feed available today (which is normally a completely balanced diet) certainly enables the birds to mature sooner than when they were reared on food which undoubtedly was lacking in protein. Very often the early-hatched birds were only just about ready by mid-November but today quite late-hatched ones are mature a month earlier.

Even the large shoots begin the season earlier than in the old days. Pre-war it was usually the last weekend in November before the woods echoed to the barrage of shots and the tapping of the beater's sticks, and really large bags were obtained by the sporting gentlemen of those times.

On the estate where I spent my working life, bags getting very close to 2,000 pheasants a day were normal (and expected) in the early part of the season. Numbers like that took a lot of dealing with, even when shot. It was especially important to ensure that the game was in perfect order when it was hung in the game larders, which meant it had to be treated correctly right from the time it was killed.

The game cart in those days was horse-drawn and a really ornate vehicle, in fact a regal specimen of the coachbuilder's art. Painted and decorated in the family colours, in this case dark blue and gold, it was a real picture in the autumn sunshine. It was always varnished and spruced up in the summer months by the Clerk of Works department, and even the hooks on which the game was hung were painted black. There was a roof over the numerous rails which ran the length of the cart, and there were almost 1000 hooks on which to hang the birds.

At lunch time, the game cart would wend its way to the game larder and unload, each bird being hung individually, and the cart was always brushed out so that it was free of feathers when the afternoon's sport began.

The man and his assistant, plus the wagoner, who often polished the glistening brasses whilst the cart was being unloaded, could have had very little time for their lunch and must have eaten it 'on the road'. Everything had to be done to precise order and game given the respect which was its due.

Pheasant shooting: a game wagon before lunch at Studley Royal, Yorkshire, c1901.

Most of the day's bag was given away: to tenants, employees and the numerous friends of the estate owner, not only locally but from one end of the country to the other. This was quite a headache for the head keeper as transport was not as readily available as now but, amazingly in a matter of a couple of days, the larders were empty and cleaned out (scrubbed with hot water to which washing soda had been added). Sometimes a brace or two had to be sent on a long journey. The legs were tied together and an addressed label tied to the necks. These gifts were then taken to the station and put on a passenger train. I wonder if they would reach their destination if this were done today?

It is really essential that any game birds should be hung by the neck as soon as possible after being shot and it is much better if they can be hung singly rather than two to a hook. Some shoots, where fairly small numbers are involved, tie them in pairs and hang them over rails on a cart. This saves time when disposing of the game later on. I prefer to see one bird to a hook especially if the weather is on the damp, warm side, as it can so easily be, even in November and December.

Many people like game to be hung for a few days before use but should hot, damp or wet pheasants be crowded together, they will very soon start to go 'green' and not very acceptable either to buy or as a gift. This effect of putting a lot of 'hot' pheasants together was brought home to me many years ago. We had caught some night poachers with only a small number of pheasants which they were carrying in a hessian sack. An hour after catching them, when hanging the birds in the larder (to be used as evidence later), it was discovered that parts of the birds were already turning green and giving off an unpleasant smell. These birds had deteriorated so much in a couple of days that they could not be used in court.

Today, under similar circumstances, the birds would have been put in a deep freeze. However, in the case described, a conviction was obtained. Perhaps the foregoing will remind rough-shooting gentlemen not to put too many birds in their game bag when wet or during humid weather, but I can hear voices saying 'The chance to get too many would be a fine thing'.

I read a letter in the local press recently, from a member of an antiblood-sports group, going through the usual drill about hunting in all its forms, and the writer was very vehement about the scarcity of hares due to the coursing meetings taking place. I will not go into his arguments about the so-called cruelty involved but it beats me how the coursing fraternity can be blamed for any shortage of hares which there may or may not be. Having being involved with one coursing club for a number of years, I always found that all the people concerned were not only dedicated to preserving hares, but were insistent that there should at all times be the minimum of cruelty. Of course, all country people following country sports have to be keen on preservation, else there would be less and less sport for them. If hares are abundant in a market-garden area, they are not at all popular with the people working the land, but in grassland areas, and even in corn-growing areas quite a high density of 'puss' can be, and is, tolerated. To blame coursing for the claimed disappearance of hares must be a misguided opinion. At any coursing meeting, very few hares are killed, often only one or two throughout the day. Should an area have lost its population of this creature, other factors must be to blame. It is more than likely a combination of a number of activities; modern farming methods for instance, must in part be responsible. Silage-making no doubt accounts for quite a few losses, not only of hares, but pheasant and partridge as well, and sprays and the widespread use of fertilisers can be detrimental to wildlife in general. The anti-blood-sports organisations are desperate to ban fox hunting; who is going to control Reynard then? There appears to have been a vast increase in the fox over the last few years. Perhaps that also, in part, accounts for any shortage of hares there might be.

I don't want these words to appear despondent, but it is absolutely essential for all people who have the conservation of our glorious countryside at heart, rural and city dwellers alike, to support one of the national organisations with these aims, such as the British Field Sports Society or British Association for Sport and Conservation. Only by joining and supporting these national organisations will the sporting activities of this great land of ours, have a chance to survive the onslaught of these 'antis'.

*   *   *

The autumn scene is such a great pleasure to the shooting man. What can be better than standing waiting for the high-flying cock pheasant as you contemplate the glories of nature around you. Today, many shooting parties are out before the foliage has really started to change colour, but there is no doubt at all that pheasants provide much better sport when the trees have shed their jackets.

The high cost of feed is partly the reason for shooting early, but there seems also to be a tendency for the smaller shoots to buy in late-hatched chicks or poults. Later-hatched birds are not going to be as mature as the early ones. Shooting them soon after the season starts in October must mean that they not only present fairly easy targets, but are also not really ready for table use. It is understandable that sportsmen with only limited cash available have to resort to such things, but I sometimes think they would get better quality sport for the same amount of money, even though it would undoubtedly mean less birds. I remember one noble lord saying to me after a shoot in November 'I killed two sky high birds at that last drive, much better than a dozen low ones'. Let's hope all sportsmen have the same attitude and don't just shoot to fill the game cart!

Quite recently a well-known member of Parliament was involved in a shooting accident on the grouse moors, when the honourable gentleman slipped as he swung onto a grouse and another gentleman and his loader were peppered with shot. The injuries were such that the loader needed hospital treatment. Now this gentleman had been shooting for years and is a competent shot and fully versed in gun handling and safety measures. Nevertheless, he slipped and two people were injured. Can the average shooting man honestly say he has never slipped with a loaded gun in his hands? It's pretty certain most of us have at one time or another, but the gun hasn't gone off, so there has been no damage.

What about the time that it does go off? Maybe no person is injured, but there is other damage, maybe to a nearby vehicle. The question then arises as to who pays for such damage and the only real answer to that is to be insured. Most shotgun owners are quite likely covered for the loss of their gun, for with the price of a good gun today this is essential. Some may assume that the ordinary household policy covers

143

Gamekeepers after a rabbit shoot, Terling, Essex, 1951.

the gun. This may not be, so it is a good idea to check. But better still, whether the gun is covered by insurance whilst in the house or not, get a policy that will also cover you whilst in the shooting field. The British Association for Sport and Conservation will be delighted to help you in this matter, so why not join?

Writing about safety in the field, I recall one occasion many years ago, when a number of men were crossing a field to go pigeon shooting. One old lad was carrying his gun on his shoulder, with the barrels parallel to the ground. He was well known to be careless in the way he handled a gun. A chap walking behind him said 'Eh, Joe, I see you use number seven shot. I prefer number six myself'. Joe said, 'I use number six, never used a number seven in me life. What are you on about?' He received the reply 'If your gun had been loaded I could have told you what size shot, take the damn thing off your shoulder and carry it "broken" under your arm'. He did so reluctantly, but it made little difference; bad habits are hard to break. Perhaps I should say that in those days the size of shot was always marked on the wad!

Talking to a retired farmer recently, he remarked on the number of rabbits in his part of the country. 'I reckon they're as thick as they were in pre-war days' he said, and went on to enthuse about the sport he hoped to have in the 'back end', when a lot of cover had gone and there were more of the conies to ground. There is a lot to be said for a day's ferreting, particularly if there are plenty of rabbits and, more important, if they are in a bolting mood. Also a pretty good day's fun can be had driving woodlands and shooting the rabbits as they cross a ride, but you need to be a good 'snap' shot for that! The farmer didn't actually invite me for a day's sport, but I must admit I had high hopes, for he said as he left 'I'll be in touch with you before long'.

It wasn't long, right enough, when he rang up, not to invite me over but to tell a tale of woe. He had gone out one evening to get a couple of three-part grown rabbits (what better to make a nice pie) which he did without much difficulty, but on his way home came across a cony which very obviously had 'myxy'. He did not think a lot of it at the time but, a day or two later, whilst out for a walk, he saw quite a number with the same trouble. The reason he had rung me was to tell me that, in no time at all, it was practically impossible to find a healthy rabbit. His hopes of 'several days' sport had been dashed and it didn't help matters when he said 'I was going to ask you over for a day'.

I expect a lot of farmers are pleased to see the rabbits cleared out by 'myxy', for a plague would be almost impossible to deal with by any other means; even to control them would be expensive but, without the odd rabbit, the countryside doesn't seem the same. Many a youngster learnt to shoot with the one-time plentiful rabbit and I bet there is many an older person who wishes there were more about!

12 · DECEMBER

WHEN THE AUTUMN FROSTS take their toll of the summer greenery, the shooting man begins to reap the harvest of the hard work put in during the spring of the year. Unless much hard work has been done, good results cannot really be expected but, even so, there are still other factors to be considered.

If a rough shoot or unkeepered syndicated shoot is some distance from the home of any of the guns, it is inevitable that the shooting will suffer. A large number of birds will be lost unless an involved person is able to give a fair amount of attention to some of the details essential to good sport.

There is no better way of holding released pheasants in a given area than by hand feeding twice a day but, of course, on most of the rough shoots and unkeepered shoots, this is almost impossible. The next best thing is a number of feed hoppers placed in the most suitable points. As the daylight hours get shorter, the natural feed has dwindled to almost nothing, so these hoppers must not be allowed to be without feed. Wheat is obviously a favourite with pheasants and, though maybe a bit more expensive than other feeds, it usually pays to use it.

Never site hoppers where they can be seen from a road or public footpath this only encourages the poaching fraternity and, on small shoots, every bird counts. If at all possible, arrange to fill the hoppers at different times of the day, or even on different days of the week; visiting woods at the same time on the same day each week makes it easier for watching eyes, with poaching in mind, to assess when it is safest to carry out a raid. Don't assume that weekends are the best times to do this routine filling of feeders. Even if it is difficult to get away to do the job during the week, it is well worth while making the effort. With so much unemployment, men with a pheasant or two in mind are able to be abroad at almost any time.

Professional gamekeepers lose pheasants to poachers, so small unkeepered shoots must accept the fact that they are going to have visitors with evil intent. Many signs are to be seen when a poaching raid has been made: bunches of pheasant feathers under the trees where birds have been knocked off the roost; strange footprints in muddy places, and, sometimes, if the poachers are careless or don't care, empty cartridge cases lying around, often of a make not used by the persons who have the shooting rights. Rifles are sometimes used and a .22 cartridge case is not easily seen, but it doesn't warrant the use of a metal detector!!

After so much labour and money has been put into the shoot, don't relax when the birds are ready to shoot. Many others are always ready to take advantage of those nice plump colourful birds strutting the stubbles.

If the feeders are concentrated in the centre of the shoot, this will help to keep the birds at home. Just because a few pheasants are seen near your boundary, do not feed there. That is much more likely to draw more of the home cover birds and lay them open to straying over the boundary and out of your reach. It is well worth while, before the shooting season starts, and even during the shooting season to walk around the boundary at every opportunity. Should any obviously hand-reared pheasants be seen, drive them back to the more central parts of the shoot. Using a dog will often be a great help, making them less inclined to return to the same place. Even a quiet drive round the roads and lanes will give you information of the movement of pheasants, which will prove most helpful when the shooting season starts.

It is the custom on many well-keepered estates, where large numbers of pheasants are reared, for guns to walk around for a day or two fairly early in the season. On these days, shooting starts at the boundary and only the pheasants that want to fly back, showing no inclination to go home, are shot. On smaller shoots a different attitude may apply. Every bird killed means a return for the earlier labours. So be it but, by and large, better sport is had later by letting birds go back to the home covers. Those birds are much more likely to provide better shooting.

Many small shoots start the season late in October, whereas large keepered shoots don't normally start until mid-November. On the small shoots, it is a good idea to leave one wood or rough area completely undisturbed if at all possible. This leaves a haven for the birds. In practice, it will be found that they will soon return to their old haunts and settle down. As the season progresses, it will often be necessary to cover the whole of the territory and, by Christmas, the birds will be a bit thin on the ground!

Is there any water on the shoot? No, not tap water! A pond or two, a small lake, or even a river can be a great asset. Anywhere in the country, this water can be used to provide at least a small amount of shooting. There may not be ducks in the area but often, by feeding these spots, wildfowl can be attracted and provide a lot of fun for the sportsman. Feed, once again, is the essential factor. Ducks are not so fussy about what they eat as pheasants, so almost any grain will attract them. Small 'chat' potatoes, preferably boiled, or practically any feed used on a farm, is quite suitable. Once again, avoid feeding in a spot which can be seen by the public. Ducks being very fond of 'dabbling' like to have some of the grain in shallow water. Feed these spots once or twice a week. It is advisable to this in the morning rather than in the evening.

You should soon have the 'quackers' coming in to feed at dusk.

This habit of feeding at night makes it most suitable for duck flighting. If you have ponds on your shoot, you are indeed lucky. After the day's pheasant shooting, why not an hour after the ducks? Say four guns, at about 25 yards from the pond, using any suitable hide, should have at least a shot or two before the light has completely faded. You must be in a position in good time because, if you are late, and the ducks are disturbed on the water, it may be too dark to see them when they return or they may seek pastures new. If you have more than one

Wildfowler putting duck decoys on a flooded meadow.

stretch of water available, don't be greedy and shoot them all the same evening. Even if you have eight guns in the shoot, it is well worth taking it in turns to flight a different stretch of water each time, once again, giving the wildlife a haven or two completely undisturbed.

If no ducks appear after feeding these flight ponds for a week or two, don't despair. There are ways of making them more attractive. One of these is putting tame, hand-reared mallard on the pond but that's a job for another season and that will be here sooner than you think.

*   *   *

December does not seem to be such an important time as it used to be to the folks who follow country pursuits. Every day of sport, be it shooting, hunting, coursing or fishing, is an important day to those taking part, so the opening statement needs qualifying. In the old days, many outdoor activities were arranged for the month of December, particularly when the young folk were home from boarding school. Today, with fast modern transport, it is possible for so many more people to take part in sport earlier in the season. It was always arranged, particularly on large estates, for a pheasant shoot to take place the weekend before Christmas. This enabled the owner of the shoot to distribute gifts of a brace of pheasants to his tenants and often to his employees. Today, with so many people having a deep freezer, it is not so important to distribute gifts of game a day or so before the festive season.

This practice of holding shoots at the right time to distribute Christmas gifts was a very important thing. Country folk have always been grateful for this largesse and looked forward to the gamekeeper arriving with a brace of plump pheasants or, in some cases, a couple of rabbits. It was usually game for the tenants and rabbits for the employees but, in either case they were always gratefully received. It was rather amusing at times, particularly where the tenant farmers were concerned. The arrival of the keeper with the game usually meant that the bottle of whisky had to come out, and farmer and keeper would sit down and, over a noggin, discuss country affairs in general.

Picker-up with pheasants slung on a Sussex game carrier.

This often led to glasses being refilled more than once, until the level of whisky in the bottle began to get rather low. Whisky in those days was 12s. 6d. a bottle (62½ p in today's money) and a brace of pheasants could be bought for a few shillings so, in many cases, it cost the farmer more for whisky than he would have had to pay for the pheasants! So much for the poor hard-up farmers. These things were important and, for that matter, are just as important today. These gifts and visits maintain a good relationship between the folks who earn their living from, and by working on, the land and the people who enjoy the sport over the land.

Many small shoots could and should look after the people they rely on so much, particularly if it is an unkeepered shoot. Don't wait until Christmas to do this or you may find that, having had a number of shoots before, you cannot get enough in mid-December to give to the people you would like to. Nevertheless don't distribute any gifts after the first shoot; no matter how early the birds were hatched, they will not be in prime condition until mid-November at the earliest. There is nothing nicer than a really plump pheasant with a nice bit of fat to keep the meat moist when cooked, but there is nothing worse than a lean skinny bird with not a shred of fat, and the meat is often dark and not very appetising. Make sure, if possible, that any gifts of birds are of good quality and don't, if you can afford it, give birds away that have both wings and both legs broken. This is a sure indication that it has been killed at too close a range and has been well and truly in the centre of shot pattern. Nobody likes to be chewing a mouthful of number six shot when having a cold pheasant 'butty'.

In the days when rabbits were really plentiful, many a happy Boxing Day was spent ferreting, usually by persons who had little opportunity to do so at other times. This brings to mind an old shepherd, a keen sportsman whose calling gave him little time to take part in country pursuits. He worked on the Home Farm and the keepers always called Boxing Day 'Tom's Day'. That was the day Tom the shepherd had a day after the conies. On the Home Farm were large poultry runs, which also had a fair number of rabbit burrows in them, and these burrows were always left undisturbed so that Tom could have a good day's sport. The poultry runs were boarded round to the height of 2 feet but, of course, the rabbits had scratched under this boarding to gain access to nearby pastures.

On Tom's big day, the first job was to go quietly round the runs and stop these holes up. Tom always made sure there were bricks close to each hole for this purpose! When all was ready, the keeper, or usually two keepers, would go to Tom's house close by and tell him when they were ready to start. A jug of cider was then produced, although on a cold day a cup of tea would have been more welcome. However, the scene was set and a start had to be made.

The ferrets were slipped quietly into the burrow and Tom stood well back with his old hammer gun at the ready, poised like the modern-day clay-pigeon shooter. Soon a rabbit appeared and Tom then went through what was another ritual of his, bringing the gun down, wiping his bushy moustache with the back of his hand, cocking the gun and then taking aim. Naturally, by now, the rabbit had gone some distance, often disappearing down another burrow, but with the holes round the poultry runs stopped up it could not escape. Tom had no chance of shooting a running cony; in fact he had no intention of doing so. He always waited for them to stop, usually by a bricked-up escape hole! After some time, the old lad had accounted for one or two and a move was made to the next burrow. Rabbits started to bolt and, after the usual procedure, several were accounted for, until one made a dash for the usual hole in the boarded run, found it closed and returned to its burrow, sitting at the entrance, no doubt realising a ferret was below ground. Tom couldn't resist this target and taking his usual steady aim fired. The rabbit jumped and with great haste made for an adjoining hole. Reloading, Tom said 'I should have got ee'. However, after waiting quite a while, it was decided to put the line ferret in and dig a rabbit or two out. Tom like to boast that he had had a day's ferreting, had so many shots and had got the same number of rabbits. Therefore, the keepers usually dug a few conies out so that the lad was at least speaking the truth, so long as he didn't say he had shot all the rabbits!

Getting to the burrow, one of the keepers said 'Hey Tom, no wonder no more bolted. Come and have a look'. There, in the hole the last rabbit had sat over, was a dead ferret, victim of Tom's last shot!

The old lad was in a terrible state 'I'll never go ferreting again. I'm going to pay for that animal' and so on. The keepers managed to placate him and, having more than one ferret with them, eventually carried on for the rest of the day. Tom did not have much to say to the other farm workers about the day's sport and it was noticeable, the next Boxing Day, that there did not seem to be the same enthusiasm as in the past.

Many such days were enjoyed throughout the country when the conies were abundant. Today, many of the younger generation would not know how to set about the pleasant task of ferreting in the proper manner.

*   *   *

Few of the younger generation know what a good day's rabbiting means. When the countryside was plagued with hordes of conies, much sport was enjoyed by working-class folk. It was practically impossible to obtain any game shooting when all large estates were preserved for their owner's pleasure, but there were always rabbits.

The farmers on these large estates usually had the rabbits off their holding but in many cases could not have a day's shooting over ferrets unless a gamekeeper was present. Thus, it was often possible for a working man keen on shooting to have a day's sport. Helping the farmer at harvest time, without pay, often led to a day's sport and quite large numbers of rabbits would be killed.

The large burrows often produced plenty of fun; he was no slouch with a gun who could kill a rabbit as it changed holes, perhaps not more than 3 yards apart! Real snap shooting that, demanding instant co-ordination of eye and muscle. Under those conditions, many a rabbit was missed. Not many rabbits that had been shot at put in a second appearance, which meant that the line ferret had to be brought into use and, in a very large burrow, a vast amount of digging was often entailed before a rabbit was unearthed.

Today an electronic device can be attached to the ferret and the ensuing 'blip' makes it possible to dig straight down to where the conies are cornered. Another of the technical advances in the countryside!

Keepers, by the very essence of their calling, had to be crafty customers and naturally looked for the easiest way when having a given area to clear of rabbits. Perhaps 'clear' is not the right word; 'reduce the numbers' would be more applicable.

The drill was to ferret all the deep burrows, not making any attempt to dig rabbits out and usually leaving the lad behind to retrieve any ferrets that were holed up. When all ferrets were accounted for, and sometimes half a dozen would be used in large burrows, the lad would lightly fill in all the holes. This process would sometimes go on for several days, but great care was taken not to go near the shallowest burrow in the area, a burrow preferably not more than a foot deep. After all surrounding areas had been ferreted, the day would come to deal with the shallow burrow. The vast majority of remaining rabbits, having deserted their homes which smelt so strongly of ferrets, would have taken up residence in the remaining untainted burrow. Often this burrow was netted and a number of rabbits, out of all proportion to the size of the burrow, would meet their doom. Once the bulk had bolted, it was an easy matter to dig the remainder out of such shallow holes.

Sometimes a long net would be run round a suitable burrow, which was often more effective than walking on the burrow to set purse nets.

Talking of long nets, this was the poacher's favourite way of catching rabbits in those distant days. Fifty years on, I don't suppose there are many long nets used, and I doubt if there is anyone as skilled in the use of them as those old-time 'visitors of the night'. It did not take a couple of men very long to run out and set 100 yards of netting. In a short while, the rabbits were driven in and the nets picked up. Using this method, the total haul, on a good night, was only limited by the number the poachers could carry!

Gamekeepers naturally didn't like to see where these operations had taken place and made efforts to apprehend the poachers. This was not really difficult because the weather and night has to be right to get a haul of conies. It was a matter of waiting for the 'visitors' where rabbits were in abundance, and being persistent should they not appear on the first night's vigil.

I remember one occasion when the writer made use of the nocturnal activities of poachers. This gang was known to operate in the area and

154

Staking out a rabbit net, 1934. Method normally used on a windy night.

expected to pay a visit on a suitable night. It so happened that orders had been received to get 100 rabbits for the following Friday. The Wednesday night was suitable for long netting and, accompanied by another keeper, I waited at a likely spot for the expected poachers. Sure enough, after not too long a wait, cycles could be heard approaching down the drive. There were three men and, as they glided past in the gloom, their bulging pockets showed that long netting was their object. We let them go, but for a reason. We knew where they were most likely to set the nets and also where they would hide their cycles. After a due space of time, we followed the route they had taken and discovered their cycles hidden in some bushes.

Now it was only a matter of waiting for the return of our 'visitors'. Some time passed but, eventually, the rustle of leaves indicated their return to their cycles. It must have been a shock to them when we stepped out and told them who we were. Fortunately, they were of the breed who accepted the fact that they would be caught sometime and showed no sign of fight. After the essential details were dealt with, we sent them on their way, minus the nets, pegs and rabbits! They had

had a good night's netting, with a bag of 86 rabbits! They would have had quite a load to carry home but, as it was past midnight, they would have draped them over their cycles as best they could. Our next day's work was made much easier with only 14 rabbits to get instead of 100!

Geese are most attractive birds. Rarely does a skein fly over, no matter how high, without our human eye trained on them. Fewer have been on the move in this area of late and I have greatly missed their honking as they passed over morning and night. These geese, mainly Canadas but with quite a number of grey lags, have lived and bred in the area for many years.

Trying to assess the reason for them being less in evidence, I came to the conclusion that the reason lies in the vast acreage of corn (wheat and barley) that has taken over from the traditional grassland. In the autumn, with such an area of literally bare soil, the geese have had to seek grazing elsewhere. They must have found a lake as well. I'm just wondering if, when the winter corn gets lush, the geese will return.

Talking to my old friend John Ruxton, who incidentally has done so much for the wild goose over the last decade or so, it appears that much the same has happened in other areas, with little detriment to the stock, at any rate of the Canada goose. We can only hope that others do not suffer after being so painstakingly established over the years.

* * *

A fair amount of game should be left in the coverts, even if several shoots have taken place over the last few weeks. Most sportsmen like to be able to provide some sport for their friends, and often teenage children, over the Christmas period. Many of today's good shots have had their first taste of game shooting during the Christmas holidays. Having enjoyed that experience, they become fanatics for the rest of their lives. There are, of course, other things to shoot as well as pheasants: duck, snipe and the humble wood pigeon.

Lucky is the lad who has the opportunity to learn to shoot on pheasants; the vast majority of shooting men have had to learn on a much humbler quarry. It is essential, no matter how a lad starts (perhaps I should also say girl, for fear of being accused of sex discrimination), that the correct way to handle a gun is instilled before ever a cartridge is put in the breech. A youngster must never forget

Rough shooter's bag: pheasant, curlew, woodcock, greylag goose. (Curlew are now on the protected list.)

that a gun is a lethal weapon and I think it says much for the shooting fraternity that there are relatively few accidents with guns.

When I first started to carry a gun as a young gamekeeper, I was told to remember one thing 'A gun is always loaded'. Of course the gun wasn't always loaded but, as long as it was treated as if it was, all would be well. I have never forgotten those words from an old keeper over 50 years ago. I hope the youngsters who are learning to shoot have as good a mentor as I had.

Clay pigeons must be the most popular way to teach an up-and-coming shot the way to handle a gun but that does not always mean it is the best way to learn to shoot. Despite the immense improvement in the clay-shooting grounds up and down the country, they do not and cannot compare with the excitement created in a young head when the pheasants start to break cover. A bird screaming overhead, speed increasing all the while, makes a greater impression on a youngster than a piece of clay disappearing into the blue. Oh, what satisfaction when that high pheasant is brought to the ground, killed clean with a single shot. I dare take a bet that every pheasant shooter remembers the first pheasant he ever shot and, if not the year, the place he killed it!

Don't think by the foregoing that clay-pigeon shooting is not useful to the sportsman. Many of the best shots sharpen up their reaction by an hour or two at the clays before the season starts in earnest. There is no reason why a youngster shouldn't get the same benefit if the clay layout is good, but a trap rigged up at home can rarely provide the targets as can the layout at a shooting school.

All you youngsters who are starting out in the shooting field for the first time, listen to your elders, learn your lessons well and you should have a lifetime of pleasure in front of you. It maybe a four-ten you are starting with but don't forget that is just as lethal as a twelve bore.

Many youngsters do not have the opportunity to start their shooting career on pheasants. In many cases, it is the pigeon that is the target. The last few years have seen a vast increase in the acreage of oil-seed rape grown. This crop is sown in the early autumn, germinates and grows quickly so that, by December, it can be 6 inches high. Just right for the ever-hungry pigeon when the weather is turning cold! Not all farmers welcome people shooting over their land, even after pigeons on rape, but by a polite and respectful approach many are only too pleased to give permission. Should any restrictions be imposed, be sure to abide by them, particularly if it is the number of guns allowed to shoot. Remember if you upset any particular farmer you won't get permission again and, more than likely nobody else will either. You can be sure the farmer will tell.

Don't leave any mess about, shut all gates and, should you see anything amiss, let the farmer know. Sometimes the farmer likes to know how many pigeons you have bagged and don't forget to ask if he wants some, they have been eating his rape anyway! It is always a wise thing to keep up a good relationship with a man who is prepared to let you shoot over his land, even if you are helping him. It is possible that there may be times when another pair of hands would come in useful. Offer to help if you can, and don't restrict your visits to the days you want to shoot a pigeon or two.

I started off by saying that there should still be a number of pheasants left in the woods. Other people will know this, and there are sure to be some of them who are poachers. You don't want to lose any to those who pass by night, whether you are in a large way or small. If you have only 100 or so birds, you are going to miss a dozen more than someone with 500 or so. I am afraid there is no certain way of stopping poaching. Many things have been tried over the years, from the old alarm gun which was set off by the intruder walking into a fine wire to the modern electronic equipment which is very expensive. Even in the old days when there were numerous gamekeepers around, and watch would be kept throughout the night, poachers would still raid a covert, so a mechanical means may give warning that someone is around but it does not catch them!

It may well be better for someone to be seen to be watching the woods, rather than that person to be waiting out of sight. Even a poacher will shy off if someone is obviously in a position to either get assistance or call the police. As a rule, rural bobbies are most helpful should they be called on when poaching is taking place. Even though you may not reside in the area where your shooting is, it can only be a good thing to make it your business to contact the local beat policeman. Should you go and watch your precious pheasants at night let the bobby know early in the season that you will be around after dark. You never know, you might even see something that will be of assistance to him but, at the same time, do not attempt to deal with a gang of poachers should you come upon them. Modern poachers can be, and in many cases are, dangerous. If you are sure they are around, either having seen them or heard shooting, don't hesitate to call the police. If a vehicle is involved, try to get the number. Write it down as soon as possible for even one letter or figure wrong makes the information useless. Adopt the method of observe not approach, and never call the police unless you are sure poaching is taking place.

Best wishes to all my readers, have a good Christmas and straight barrels!